MW00940362

Concordance

+ + + + + + + + + + + +

Concordance

(King James Version)

THE LESSONS -

How to Understand Spiritual Principles, Spiritual Activities, and Rising Emotions

+ + +

Reverend Sandra Casey-Martus, MEd, MTS
and Carla R. Mancari, MEd

+ + + + + + + + + + + +

Copyright © 2008 by Reverend Sandra Casey-Martus, MEd, MTS and Carla R. Mancari, MEd.

ISBN: Softcover   978-1-4363-7205-3

All rights reserved. No part of this concordance may be reproduced or retransmitted in any form or by no means without the written permission of the Authors.

The Scripture quotations contained herein are from the Holy Bible, King James Version. Cambridge University Press Bentley House, 200 Euston Road, London NW1 2 DB American Branch: 32 East 57th Street, New York, N.Y. 10022.

This book was printed in the United States of America.

To order additional copies of this book, contact:
Xlibris Corporation
1-888-795-4274
www.Xlibris.com
Orders@Xlibris.com
53566

CONTENTS

THE NEW TESTAMENT—CONCORDANCE

THE OLD TESTAMENT—CONCORDANCE

The Reverend Sandra Casey-Martus, is the Associate Rector of All Saints' Episcopal Church in Austin, Texas. She served as Vicar of St. Francis of the Tetons Episcopal Church and Director of the Alta Retreat Center in Alta, Wyoming from 1994-2005.

An adjunct faculty member of the Episcopal Seminary of the Southwest, Sandy spent ten years on Contemplative Outreach Ltd's Formation Training and Retreat Service teams. Her Article, "Centering Prayer and Priestly Formation" appears in Continuum Press's publication *Centering Prayer in daily life and Ministry,* 1998 and she is the co-author of *The Lessons, 2008.*

Sandy holds a BS and MEd from Springfield College, Massachusetts, an MTS. from Oblate School of Theology, and a CITS from the Episcopal Seminary of Southwest.

Sandy is the co-founder of the Contemplative Invitation Teaching and has studied various forms of contemplative prayer for over thirty years. Presently, with her priestly service, she writes, travels, teaches the Christ Centered Prayer practice, and leads Christian contemplative prayer retreats.

Teacher and spiritual director Carla R. Mancari had her first transcendent experience in 1973 while visiting a shrine in Lourdes, France. Working at the time as a Counselor, she immediately resigned and began a spiritual quest. Carla traveled all over the world studying with Christian, Buddhist, and Hindu Masters.

Carla's Spiritual truth-seeking ultimately brought her into an on-going intimate personal relationship with Jesus Christ. She has taught Christ-Centered Spiritual Principles and silent prayer for over 30 years.

Carla is the author, *Walking on the Grass, A White Woman In A Black World* and co-author of *The Lessons, 2008.* She cofounder of the Contemplative Invitation Teaching. In addition to holding a BA from the University of South Carolina, Columbia, and an MEd from South Carolina State University, she was certified as a counseling psychologist.

FORWARD

The concordance provides a cross reference of the scriptures and topics making access to the *Lessons* material speedy and efficient.

You may quickly identify, locate, and cross reference all of the material contained within *The Lessons.*

Brief commentary phrases of the individual 207 Lessons are included as a guide and reminder of *The Lessons* content.

The Concordance is the perfect companion and an invaluable tool when working with and studying *The Lessons.*

ACKNOWLEDGMENT

We are especially grateful to Irene Landers for her artistic contribution making the covers for *The Lessons* and the *Concordance*.

Our appreciation for all of the students who have embraced the Christ Centered Prayer practice. It is their work with *The Lessons* that suggested a *Concordance* would be helpful.

THE CONCORDANCE SCRIPTURE VERSE/S ARE IN THE FOLLOWING FORMAT:

1. Book (**MATTHEW, MARK**, etcetera) upper left corner of each page

2. Chapter and verse/s, excerpt of text

3. LESSON number, title, Student's Story (when included in a LESSON), and a LESSON commentary

4. LESSON page number

5. Number, Letter, or Definition within the LESSON

EXAMPLE:

MATTHEW:

6:19 "Lay not up for yourselves," LESSON: 5 (Student's Story)—AWARENESS - CONSCIOUSNESS—The Changeless, Individual Expressions, Page 10 - #26, Letter, or Definition.

Number or letter may not always be found on same page where a Lesson begins. Definition is found immediately after the LESSON's title.

THE NEW TESTAMENT

(KING JAMES VERSION)

MATTHEW:

2:13 "Arise and take the young child and his mother, and flee into Egypt," LESSON: 150—SACRED & SECRET—Protective Environment, Page 168 - #4.

3:2 "And saying, Repent ye: for the Kingdom of Heaven is at hand," LESSON: 99—KINGDOM—Natural Inheritance, #3 - Page 119 - #3.

3:11 "I indeed baptize you with water . . . he that cometh after me is mightier," LESSON: 24—BAPTISM—Water and Spirit Invitation, Page 40 - #4.

3:17 "And lo a voice from heaven, This is my beloved son," LESSON: 44—CONTEMPLATIVE—Accepts the Invitation, Page 60 - #8 & LESSON: 116 (Student's Story)—OBEDIENCE—Establishing A Balance, Page 137 - #17.

4:4 "It is written, Man shall not live by bread alone," LESSON: 78—GRATITUDE—Standing on Holy Ground, Page 99 - #3.

4:7 "Thou shall not tempt the Lord thy God," LESSON: 49 (Student's Story)—DESIRES AND TEMPTATIONS—Distractions, Page 64 - #2.

4:19 "Follow Me, I will make you fisher of men," LESSON: 2—AN INVITATION—Come Follow Me, Page 7 - Definition.

5:8 "Blessed are the pure in heart," LESSON: 4—SPIRITUAL HEART CENTER—Best Kept Secret, Page 9 - #7 & LESSON: 11—PURIFICATION PROCESS—Spiritual House Cleaning, Page 22 - Definition & LESSON: 113—MOTIVATION—Rising Interest, Page 135 - #6.

MATTHEW:

5:11-12 "Blessed are ye, when *men* shall revile you," LESSON: 126—POSITION—Specific Job Title and Service, Page 146 - #10.

5:14 "Ye are the light of the world" LESSON: 152—SENSITIVITY—Personal Acceptance of Criticism, Page 169 - #9.

5:16 "Let your light so shine before men," LESSON: 40—CONFIDENCE—Total Trust, Page 57 - #4 & LESSON: 53 (Student's Story)—DISCIPLESHIP—Accepting the Hand of Jesus, Page 69 - #2.

5:48 "Be ye perfect therefore, even as your Father," LESSON: 82—HEALTH - SPIRITUAL—State of Wholeness, Page 104 - #6 & LESSON: 78—GRATITUDE—Standing On Holy Ground, Page 99 - #4 & LESSON: 163—SOUL PAIN—Dark Days and Darker Nights, 180 - #10.

6:1 "Take heed that ye do not your alms before me," LESSON: 113—MOTIVATION—Rising Interest, Page 135 - #4.

6:2 "Therefore when thou doest *thine* alms, do not sound a trumpet before thee," LESSON: 113—MOTIVATION—Rising Interest, 135 - #7.

6:3 "But when thou doest alms let not thou left hand know what your right hand is doing," LESSON: 113—MOTIVATION—Rising Interest, 135 - #8.

6:4 "That thine alms may be in secret," LESSON: 53 (Student's Story)—DISCIPLESHIP—Accepting the Hand of Jesus, Page 69 - #10 & LESSON: 113—MOTIVATION—Rising Interest, Page 135 - #9.

6:6 "But when thou prayest, enter into thy closet," LESSON:70—FLEXIBILITY—Freedom to Adjust, Page 92 - #6 & LESSON: 149—RETREAT CENTER—Spiritual Renewal, Page 167 - #7.

6:8 "Be not therefore like unto them," LESSON: 8—ATTRACTION—Manifestations of Vibrating Energy, Page 17 - #18 & LESSON 39—CONCENTRATION—One Pointedness, Page 55 - #11 & LESSON: 108—LOVING - DIVINE—God In Action, Page 131 - #4.

MATTHEW:

6:9-13 "After this manner therefore pray ye," LESSON: 131—PRAYING - PRAYERS—Hail Mary, Lord's Prayer, Rosary, Page 150 - **THE LORD'S PRAYER: A.**

6:10 "Thy Kingdom come, thy will be done," LESSON: 39— CONCENTRATION—One Pointedness, #16—Page 55 & LESSON: 198—WILL - FREE—Concentrated Mental Energy, Page 214 - #8.

6:12 & 6:15 "And forgive us our debts . . . But if ye forgive not men," LESSON: 10—FORGIVENESS—Not Easy To Comprehend, Page 21 - #4.

6:14 "For if ye forgive men their trespasses," LESSON: 131— PRAYING - PRAYERS—Hail Mary, Lord's Prayer, Rosary, Page 150 - **LORD'S PRAYER: H.**

6:19 "Lay not up for yourselves," LESSON: 5 (Student's Story)— AWARENESS - CONSCIOUSNESS—The Changeless, Individual Expressions, Page 10 - #26.

6:24 "No one can serve two masters," LESSON: 69—FEAR—Stumbling Block, Page 91 - #14.

6:25 "Take no thought for your life," LESSON: 39—CONCENTRATION— One Pointedness, Page 55 - #5 & LESSON: 101—LAYERS—Three Major Layers, Page 121 - **PHYSICAL SENSE LAYER: B.** & LESSON: 168 (Student's Story)—SUPPLY—Spiritual Principle, Page 185 - #6.

6:26 "Behold the fowls of the air," LESSON:168 (Student's Story)— SUPPLY—Spiritual Principle, Page 185 - #14.

6:27 "Which of you by taking thought," LESSON: 27 (Student's Story)— BODY—Temple - Mode of Transportation, Page 42 - #14 & LESSON: 39—CONCENTRATION—One Pointedness, Page 55 - #4 & LESSON: 168 (Student's Story)—SUPPLY—Spiritual Principle, Page 185 - #10.

6:31 "Therefore take no thought," LESSON: 8—ATTRACTION— Manifestations of Vibrating Energy, Page 17 - #20.

MATTHEW:

6:32 "for your heavenly Father knoweth that ye have need of all these things," LESSON: 168 (Student's Story)—SUPPLY - Spiritual Principle, Page 185 - #11.

6:33 "But seek ye first the Kingdom of God," LESSON: 39—CONCENTRATION—One Pointedness, Page 55 - #6 & LESSON: 50 (Student's Story)—DETACHMENT—Freedom From Suffering, Page 66 - #16 & LESSON: 69—FEAR—Stumbling Block, Page 91 - #11 & LESSON: 168 (Student's Story)—SUPPLY—Spiritual Principle, Page 185 - Definition.

7:1 "Judge not, that ye be not judged," LESSON: 41—CONSCIENCE—Conditioned-Right or Wrong, Page 58 - #8 & LESSON: 98—JUDGING—To Bring Into Question, Page 119 - #1.

7:7 "Ask and it shall be given you," LESSON 39—CONCENTRATION - One Pointedness, Page 55 - #15.

7:13 "broad *is* the way that leadeth to destruction," LESSON: 3—STRAIGHT GATE AND NARROW WAY—The Direct Path, Page 8 - #11 & LESSON: 49 (Student's Story)—DESIRES AND TEMPTATIONS—Distractions, Page 64 - #10.

7:14 "Because strait is the gate and narrow is the way," LESSON: 3—STRAIGHT GATE AND NARROW WAY—The Direct Path, Page 8 - #1 & LESSON: 13 (Student's Story)—CHRIST CENTERED PRAYER—The Method, Page 24 - #13 & LESSON: 157—SIGN OF THE CROSS—More Then a Symbol, Page 175 - #5.

7:20 "Wherefore by their fruits ye shall know them," LESSON: 165—SPIRITUAL DIRECTORS—Inner and Outer Guidance, Page 181 - #10.

7:21 "Not every one that saith unto me, Lord, Lord, shall enter into the kingdom of heaven," LESSON: 43—CONSENT—Love's Wisdom, Page 59 - Definition.

MATTHEW:

7:29 "For he taught them as *one* having authority, and not as the scribes," LESSON 152—SENSITIVITY—Personal Acceptance of Criticism, Page 170 - #8.

8:13 "Go thy way; and as thou hast believed, *so* be it done unto thee," LESSON: 187 (Student's Story)—VIRGINAL CONCEPTION—Conception of Jesus, Page 204 - #5.

9:29 "Then touched he their eyes," LESSON: 66—FAITH—The Kingdom of God, Page 87 - #3.

10:14 "whosoever shall not receive you, nor hear your words," LESSON: 152—SENSITIVITY—Personal Acceptance of Criticism, 170 - #6.

10:33 "But whosoever shall deny me before men, him will I also deny before my Father which is in heaven," LESSON 152—SENSITIVITY—Personal Acceptance of Criticism, 170 - #7.

10:38 "And he that taketh not his cross, and followeth after me, is not worthy of me," LESSON: 157—SIGN OF THE CROSS—More Then a Symbol, 175 - #10.

10:39 "He that findeth his life shall lose it," LESSON: 50 (Student's Story)—DETACHMENT—Freedom from Suffering, Page 66 - #3 & LESSON: 178 (Student's Story)—TRUST I—In The Christ, Page 193 - #5.

10:40 "He that receiveth you receiveth me, and he that receiveth me receiveth him that sent me," LESSON: 154 (Student's Story)—SERVANT I—The Christ Servant, 171 - #7.

11:5 "The blind receive their sight," LESSON: 81—HEALING—Truth Revealed, Page103 - Definition.

11:28 "Come unto me, all ye that labor and are heavy laden," LESSON: 2—AN INVITATION—Come Follow Me, Page 7 - #5 & LESSON 50 (Student's Story)—DETACHMENT—Freedom from suffering, Page

MATTHEW:

66 - #13 & LESSON: 76—GIFTS—Necessary Assistance, Page 98 - **GIFTS TO AWAKEN YOU:** D & LESSON: 91—IMPATIENCE—Pressing Against the Gates of Heaven, Page 112 - #8.

11:29 "Come unto me, all *ye* that labour," LESSON: 20—ANALYZING—Mind/Intellect's Nature, Page 37 - #7.

11:30 "For my yoke *is* easy," LESSON 50 (Student's Story)—DETACHMENT—Freedom From Suffering, Page 66 - #13.

12:36-37 "That every idle word that men shall speak . . . For by thy words thou shall be justified," LESSON: 35—COMPANY—Those With Whom You Relate Well, Page 52 - #8 & LESSON: 158—SILENCE - OUTER & INNER—The Still Small Voice, Page 176 - **OUTER SILENCE:** #3.

12:50 "For whosoever shall do the will of my Father which is in heaven, the same is my brother, and sister, and mother," LESSON: 146—RELATIONSHIPS—Family, Friends, and Strangers, Page 164 - #12.

13:9 "Who hath ears to hear, let him hear, "LESSON: 32—CHANGE - CONVERSION—The Inevitable, Page 48 - #1.

13:55 "Is not this the carpenter's son?," LESSON: 126—POSITION—Specific Job Title and Service, Page 146 - #8.

13:57 "A prophet is not without honour, save in his own country," LESSON: 126—POSITION—Specific Job Title and Service, Page 146 - #16.

16:19 "I will give unto thee the keys of the kingdom of heaven," LESSON: 14 (Student's Story)—POWER PRAYER—The Method, Page 27 - #5 & LESSON: 49 (Student's Story)—DESIRES AND TEMPTATION—Distractions, Page 64 - #11.

16:24-25 "If any *man* will come after me, let him deny himself . . . For whosoever will save his life shall lose it," LESSON 122—PERSECUTION AND CRUCIFIXION, Page 143 - **CRUCIFIXION:** E & LESSON 152—SENSITIVITY—Personal Acceptance of Criticism, Page 169 - #9 & LESSON: 157—SIGN OF THE

MATTHEW:

CROSS—More Then a Symbol, Page 175 - #3 & LESSON: 163—SOUL PAIN—Dark Days and Darker Nights, Page 180 - #4.

16:26 "For what is a man profited," LESSON: 8—ATTRACTION—Manifested Vibrating Energy, Page 17 - #9 & LESSON: 135—PRIDE—Comes Before A Fall, Page 156 - #16.

18:4 "Whosoever therefore shall humble himself as this little child," LESSON: 87 (Student's Story)—HUMILITY—What Can I Do Myself? Page 108 - #6 & LESSON 135—PRIDE, Page 156 - **OVERCOMING FALSE PRIDE:** B.

18:22 "Until seventy times seven" LESSON:10—FORGIVENESS—Not Easy To Comprehend, Page 21 - Definition.

19:11 "All *men* cannot receive this saying," LESSON: 30 (Student's Story)—CELIBACY—Abstention of Sexual Energy, Page 46 - #5.

16:19 "I will give unto thee the keys to the kingdom of heaven," LESSON: 14 (Student's Story)—POWER PRAYER—The Method, Page 27 - #5.

19:26 "With men this is impossible," LESSON:29—CAN'T—Good Excuse, Never a Good Reason, Page 45 - #5.

21:13 "My house shall be called a house of prayer," LESSON: 205—X-MAS-CHRISTMAS—Sacred Remembrance, Page 219 - #8.

22:29-30 "Ye do err, not knowing the scriptures . . . For in the resurrection they neither marry, or are given in marriage," LESSON: 143—REFLECTION—God's Image, Page 163 - #7.

22:37 "love thy Lord thy God with all thy heart," LESSON: 4—SPIRITUAL HEART CENTER—Best Kept Secret, Page 9 - #5 & LESSON: 78—GRATITUDE—Standing on Holy Ground, Page 99 - #11.

22:37-40 "love thy Lord thy God waith all thy heart and the second *is* like unto it. On these two commandment hang all the law and the

MATTHEW:

prophets," LESSON: 62—EVIL—Self-Inflecting, Page 82 - #7 & LESSON: 107—LOVE-GOD's—God's Nature, Page 130 - #10 & LESSON: 133—PRESENCE—The Spirit of Jesus, 154 - #3.

22:39 "love thy neighbor as thy self," LESSON: 5—AWARENESS - CONSCIOUSNESS (Student's Story)—The Changeless, Individual Expressions, Page 10 - #20.

23:37 "O Jerusalem, Jerusalem, *thou* that killest the prophets . . . how often would I have gathered thy children together," LESSON: 105—LONELINESS—That God Forsaken Feeling, Page 127 - #13 & LESSON 152—SENSITIVITY—Personal Acceptance of Criticism, Page 169 - #13.

25:40 "In as much as ye have done *it* to the least of these," LESSON: 27 (Student's Story)—BODY—Temple - Mode of Transportation, Page 42 - #11.

26:11 "For ye have the poor always with you," LESSON:45—CONTRADICTIONS—Inner-Outer Conflicts, Page 61 - #14.

26:39 "went a little further and fell on his face," LESSON: 33 (Student's Story)—CHOICES & DECISIONS—Selection - Carry Through, Page 50 - #7 & LESSON: 43—CONSENT—Love's Wisdom, Page 59 - #1 & LESSON: 87—HUMILITY—What Can I Do Myself?, Page 108 - #13 & LESSON: 113—MOTIVATION—Rising Interest, Page 135 - #2 & LESSON: 122—PERSECUTION AND CRUCIFIXION—Initiations, Page 143 - **PERSECUTION:** C. & LESSON 173—TEARS - CRYING, Page 190 - #7 & LESSON: 198—WILL - FREE—Concentrated Mental Energy, Page 214 - #7.

26:41 "Watch and pray that ye enter not into temptation," LESSON: 55 (Student's Story)—DRAMA—Hyper-Response/ Reaction, Page 73 - #5.

26:42 "O my Father, if this cup may not pass away from me," LESSON 122—PERSECUTION - CRUCIFIXION—False Sense and Giving It Up, Page 143 - **PERSECUTION:** D.

MATTHEW:

26:70 & 26:72 "But he denied before *them* all, saying, I know not what thou sayest . . . And again he denied with an oath," LESSON: 152—SENSITIVITY - Personal Acceptance of Criticism, Page169 - #1 & LESSON: 145—REJECTING - REALITY—Intentionally Turning Away, Page 164 - #11.

27:46 "My God, my God, why hast thou forsaken me?," LESSON: 32—CHANGE - CONVERSION—The Inevitable, Page 48 - #10.

28:20 "And lo, I am with you always," LESSON: 106 (Student's Story)— LONGING—Inner Yearning, Page 128 - **STUDENT'S STORY** - Paragraph 4 & LESSON: 121—PENTECOST—Holy Spirit Reality, Page 142 - #3 & LESSON: 191—VULNERABLE—False Sense of Separation, Page 209 - #3.

* * *

14

MARK:

4:12 "That seeing they may see, and not perceive; and hearing they may hear, and not understand," LESSON: 159—SIN—False Concept, Page 177 - #1.

6:31 "Come ye yourselves apart into a desert place, and rest a while," LESSON: 149—RETREAT CENTER—Spiritual Renewal, Page167 - #8.

7:9 "Full well you reject ye the commandment of God, that ye may keep your own tradition," LESSON: 145—REJECTING - REALITY—Intentionally Turning Away, Page 164 - #6.

8:18 "Having eyes, see ye not?," LESSON: 126—POSITION—Specific Job Title and Service, Page 146 - #14.

9:23 "If thou canst believe, all things *are* possible," LESSON: 95—INSPIRATION—Colors the Black and White Pictures of Life, Page116 - #9.

10:6 "God made them male and female," LESSON: 162—SOUL—Breath of God, Page 179 - #6.

10:9 "What therefore God hath joined together, let not man put asunder," LESSON: 109—MARRIAGE—Fluid Occurrence On Plane of Opposites, Page 132 - #4.

12:29-31 "And the second *is* like, namely this, Thou shalt love thy neighbour as thyself," LESSON: 31—CHARITY—God's Love Expansively Expressed, Page 48 - #3 & LESSON: 5 (Student's Story)—AWARENESS - CONSCIOUSNESS—The Changeless, Individual

MARK:

Expressions, Page 10 - #19 & LESSON: 36—COMPARING—Paper Credentials, Page 53 - #2.

12:30 "And thou shalt love the Lord thy God with all thy heart, and with all thy soul," LESSON: 162—SOUL—Breath of God, Page 179 - #4.

12:32 "for there is one God; and there is none other but he," LESSON: 143—REFLECTION—God's Image, Page 163 - #6 & LESSON:187 (Student's Story)—VIRGINAL CONCEPTION—Conception of Jesus, Page 204 - #4 & LESSON: 191 (Student's Story)—VULNERABLE— False Sense of Separation, Page 209 - #5 & LESSON: 203— WORDS - WRITTEN - SPOKEN—Manifestation of Thoughts, Page 218 - #7.

14:38 "Watch ye and pray, lest ye enter into temptation," LESSON: 131—PRAYING - PRAYERS—Hail Mary, Lord's Prayer, Rosary: Hail Mary, Page 150 - **THE LORD'S PRAYER:** J.

15:34 "My God, my God, why hast thou forsaken me?," LESSON:105— LONELINESS—That God Forsaken Feeling, Page 127 - #5 & LESSON: 163—SOUL PAIN—Dark Days and Darker Nights, Page 180 - #7.

*　　*　　*

LUKE:

1:27-28 "And the angel came in unto her, and said, Hail, *thou that art* highly favoured," LESSON: 131—PRAYING - PRAYERS—Hail Mary, Lord's Prayer, Rosary, Page 150 - **HAIL MARY:** A.

1:35 "The Holy Ghost shall come upon thee," LESSON: 131—PRAYING - PRAYERS—Hail Mary, Lord's Prayer, and Rosary, Page 150 - **HAIL MARY:** B.

1:37 "For with God nothing shall be impossible," LESSON: 53 (Student's Story)—DISCIPLESHIP—Accepting the Hand of Jesus, Page 69 - #7.

1:38 "be it unto me according to thy word," LESSON: 43—CONSENT—Love's Wisdom, Page 59 - #7 & LESSON 131—PRAYING - PRAYERS—Hail Mary, Lord's Prayer, and the Rosary, Page 150 - **HAIL MARY:** C. & LESSON: 187 (Student's Story)—VIRGINAL CONCEPTION—Conception of Jesus, Page 204 - #6.

1:46-47 "My soul doth magnify the Lord," LESSON: 112—MOTHER MARY - SPIRIT OF MARY—Patient Guidance, Page 134 - #1.

4:4 "Man shall not live by bread alone," LESSON: 72—FOOD—Medicine for the Body, Page 93 - #7.

4:5 "taking him up into an high mountain, shewed unto him all the kingdoms of the world in a moment of time," LESSON: 110—MEMORY - RECALL—In the Present, Page 133 - #10.

LUKE:

4:8 "Get thee behind me, Satan!," LESSON: 152—SENSITIVITY—Personal Acceptance of Criticism, Page 169 - #12 & LESSON: 198—WILL - FREE—Concentrated Mental Energy, Page 214 - #3.

4:18-19 "The Spirit of the Lord is upon me," LESSON: 53 (Student's Story)—DISCIPLESHIP—Accepting the Hand of Jesus, Page 69 - Definition.

8:15 "But that on the good ground are they, which in an honest and good heart, having heard the word, keep *it,* and bring forth fruit with patience," LESSON: 119—PATIENCE—Staying In Place, Page 141 - #12.

9:59 "An he said unto another, Follow me," LESSON: (Student's Story) 61—EUCHARIST—Gift of Remembrance, Page 81 - #8.

9:62 "No man, having put his hand to the plough, and looking back, is fit for the kingdom of God," LESSON: 145—REJECTING - REALITY—Intentionally Turning Away, Page164 - #2 & LESSON: 182—TRYING—Built in Failure, Page 199 - #8.

12:20 "*thou* fool this night thy soul shall be required of thee," LESSON: 38—COMPLACENCY—Satisfied With the Distance Traveled, Page 55 - #5.

12:28 "If God so clothe the grass, which is to day in the field," LESSON: 66—FAITH—The Kingdom of God, Page 87 - #5.

12:31 "But rather seek ye the kingdom of God," LESSON: 66—FAITH—The Kingdom of God, Page 87 - #5.

12:32 "Fear not little flock," LESSON 26—BIRTH-DEATH—Imaginary Cycle, Page 41- #9.

12:48 "For unto whomsoever much is given, of him shall be much required," LESSON: 67 (Student's Story)—FAITHFULNESS—Standing Firm, Page 87 - #5.

LUKE:

12:51 "Suppose ye that I am come to give peace on earth?," LESSON: 126—POSITION—Specific Job Title and Service, Page 146 - #12.

14:18 "And they all with one *consent* began to make excuse," LESSON: 23—AVOIDANCE—Turning Away, Page 39 - #3.

14:24 "For I say unto you, that none of those men which were bidden shall taste of my supper," LESSON: 23—AVOIDANCE—Turning Away, Page 39 - #3.

15:4-5 "What man of you, having an hundred Sheep, if he lose one of them, doth not leave the ninety and nine in the wilderness, and go after that which is lost," LESSON: 78—GRATITUDE—Standing on Holy Ground, Page 99 - #9.

15:31 "Son thou art ever with me," LESSON: 69—FEAR—Stumbling Block, Page 91 - #7 & LESSON: 76—GIFTS—Necessary Assistance, Page 98 - #6 & LESSON: 191 (Student's Story)—VULNERABLE—False Sense of Separation, Page 209 - #2.

17:9-10 "Doth he thank that servant because he did the things that were commanded him?" LESSON: 126—POSITION—Specific Job Title and Service, Page 146 - #11.

17:20-21 "The kingdom of God cometh without observation," LESSON: 26—BIRTH - DEATH—Imaginary Cycle, Page 41 - #8 & LESSON: 39—CONCENTRATION—One Pointedness, Page 55 - #14 & LESSON: 96 (Student's Story)—JESUS - PRE-EXISTENCE - PERSONAL - IMPERSONAL, Page 116 - **PRE-EXISTENCE:** E. & LESSON: 99—KINGDOM—Natural Inheritance, Page 119 - #6 & LESSON: 131—PRAYING - PRAYERS—Hail Mary, Lord's Prayer, and Rosary, Page 150 - **LORD'S PRAYER:** K.

20:13 "I will send my beloved son," LESSON: 25—BELOVED—The One in the Many, Page 41 - #9.

LUKE:

20:35-36 "they which shall be accounted worthy to obtain that world, and the resurrection from the dead, neither marry, nor are given in marriage," LESSON: 148—RESURRECTION - ASCENSION—Overcoming & Returning Home, Page 166 - #2.

21:19 "In your patience posses ye your souls," LESSON 119—PATIENCE— Staying In Place, Page 141 - #14.

22:19-20 "he took bread and gave thanks," LESSON: 61 (Student's Story)—EUCHARIST—Gift of Remembrance, Page 81 - Definition.

22:29 "I appoint unto you a kingdom," LESSON: 44—CONTEMPLATIVE— Accepts the Invitation, Page 60 - #1 & LESSON: 76—GIFTS—Necessary Assistance, Page 98 - #5.

22:42 "Father, if thou be willing, remove this cup from me," LESSON: 69—FEAR—Stumbling Block, Page 91 - #15 & LESSON: 178 (Student's Story)—TRUST I—In The Christ, Page 193 - Definition & LESSON: 198—WILL - FREE—Concentrated Mental Energy, Page 214 - #5.

23:34 "Father, forgive them," LESSON: 62—EVIL—Self-Inflecting, Page 82 - #4 & LESSON: 126—POSITION—Specific Job Title and Service, Page 146 - #18.

23:43 "Verily I say unto thee, To day shalt thou be with me in paradise," LESSON 26—BIRTH - DEATH—Imaginary Cycle, Page 41 - #10 & LESSON: 141(Student's Story)—RECONCILE - ATONEMENT - SALVATION— Acceptance, Page 159 - #8.

24:49 "but tarry ye in the city of Jerusalem, until ye be endued with power from on high," LESSON: 121—PENTECOST—Holy Spirit Reality, Page 142 - #1.

*   *   *

JOHN:

1:1-5 "In the beginning was the Word, and the Word was with God. All things were made by him; and without him was not any thing made that was made. In him was life; and the life was the light of men," LESSON: 13 (Student's Story)—CHRIST CENTERED PRAYER Method, Page 24 - #2 & LESSON: 96 (Student's Story)—JESUS-PRE-EXISTENCE-PERSONAL-IMPERSONAL, Page 116 - **1. PRE-EXISTENCE:** D. & LESSON 148—RESURRECTION - ASCENSION—Overcoming & Returning Home, Page 166 - **ASCENSION:** #8 & LESSON: 187 (Student's Story)—VIRGINAL CONCEPTION—Conception of Jesus, Page 204 - #9.

1:3-4 "All things were made by him, and without him was not anything made," LESSON: 27 (Student's Story)—BODY—Temple - Mode of Transportation, Page 42 - Definition & LESSON: 47—CREATION—In the Light of Awareness, Page 62 - #10.

1:4-5 "In him was life; and the life was the light of men," LESSON: 126—POSITION—Specific Job Title and Service, 146 - #15 & LESSON: 152—SENSITIVITY—Personal Acceptance of Criticism, Page 169 - #2.

1:14 "the word was made flesh and dwelt among us," LESSON: 13 (Student's Story)—CHRIST CENTERED PRAYER—Method, Page 24 - #3 & LESSON: 100—LANGUAGE—Expressions of Communication, Page 120 - **2. SPOKEN WORD:** A.

1:16 "And of his fulness have all we received, and grace for grace," LESSON: 77—GRACE—Light of Awareness, Page 99 - #6.

JOHN:

3:6 "What is born of the flesh is flesh," LESSON: 123—PERSON—A Separative False Sense of Reality, Page 144 - Definition.

3:13 "no man hath ascended up to heaven, but he that came down from heaven," LESSON 148—RESURRECTION - ASCENSION—Overcoming & Returning Home, **ASCENSION:** Page 166 - #1.

4:24 "God *is* a Spirit," LESSON: 26—BIRTH - DEATH—Imaginary Cycle, Page 41 - #2 & LESSON: 131—PRAYING - PRAYERS—Hail Mary, Lord's Prayer, Rosary, Page 150 - **LORD'S PRAYER:** E. & LESSON: 204—WORSHIP—Spiritual Falling to Your Knees, Page 219 - Definition.

4:32 "I have meat to eat that ye know not of," LESSON: 152—SENSITIVITY—Personal Acceptance of Criticism, Page 169 - #5.

5:14 "Behold, thou art made whole: sin no more," LESSON: 159—SIN—False Concept, Page 177 - #6.

5:24 "He that heareth my word, and believeth on him that sent me, hath everlasting life," LESSON: 188—VOCABULARY—Subjected to Change, Page 205 - #6.

5:30 "I can do nothing on my own," LESSON: 3—STRAIGHT GATE AND NARROW WAY—The Direct Path, Page 8 - #4.

6:10-12 "When Jesus multiplied the loaves of fishes," LESSON: 66—FAITH—The Kingdom of God, Page 87 - #2.

6:15 "he departed again into the mountain," LESSON 66—FAITH—The Kingdom of God, Page 87 - #4.

6:26 "Ye seek me, not because ye saw the miracles," LESSON: 126—POSITION—Specific Job Title and Service, Page 146 - #7.

6:35 "I am the bread of life," LESSON: 72—FOOD—Medicine for the Body, Page 93 - #6 & LESSON: 178 (Student's Story)—TRUST I—In The Christ, Page 193 - #9.

JOHN:

6:38 "I came down from heaven, not to do mine own will but the will of him that sent me," LESSON: 131—PRAYING - PRAYERS—Hail Mary, Lord's Prayer, and Rosary, Page 150 - **LORD'S PRAYER:** D.

6:63 "It is the spirit that quickeneth," LESSON: 186—VANITY—Unnecessary Attention to the Physical Appearance, Page 203 - #5.

6:69 "we believe and are sure that thou art that Christ," LESSON: 140—RECOGNITION—JESUS' PRESENCE—Signs, Page 159 - #5.

7:24 "Judge not according to the appearances," LESSON: 27 (Student's Story)—BODY—Temple - Mode of Transportation, Page 42 - #9.

7:17 "If any man will do his will, he shall know of the doctrine," LESSON: 99—KINGDOM—Natural Inheritance, Page 119 - #1.

8:23 "Ye are from beneath; I am from above," LESSON: 192—WAKING UP—Returning Home, Page 210 - #8.

8:31-32 "If ye continue in my word, *then* ye are my disciples indeed; and ye shall know the truth and the truth shall make you free," LESSON: 104—LISTENING—Guidance from the Spiritual Heart Center, Page 126 - #3.

8:32 "the truth shall make you free," LESSON: 8—ATTRACTION—Manifestations of Vibrating Energy, Page 17 - #22 & LESSON: 181—TRUTH—Revealed Teaching, Page 198 - #10.

9:5 "As long as I am in the world, I am the light of the world," LESSON: 78—GRATITUDE—Standing On Holy Ground, Page 99 - #14.

10:7 "I am the door of the sheep," LESSON: 3—STRAIGHT GATE AND NARROW WAY—The Direct Path, Page 8 - Definition.

10:09 "I am the door: if any man enter in, he shall be saved," LESSON: 13 (Student's Story)—CHRIST CENTERED PRAYER—Method, Page 24 - #16

JOHN:

& LESSON: 101—LAYERS—Three Major Layers, Page 121 - **SPIRITUAL LAYER:** #4.

10:10 "I am come that they might have life, and that they might have *it* more abundantly," LESSON: 78—GRATITUDE—Standing On Holy Ground, Page 99 - #13.

10:30 "I and *my* Father are one," LESSON: 25—BELOVED—The One in the Many, Page 41 - Definition & LESSON: 93 (Student's Story)—INNER & OUTER—Permanence & Impermanence, Page 114 - #6 & LESSON: 96 (Student's Story)—JESUS-PRE-EXISTENCE-PERSONAL-IMPERSONAL, Page 116 - **3. IMPERSONAL: F.**

11:23-24 "Thy brother shall rise again," LESSON: 148—RESURRECTION - ASCENSION—Overcoming & Returning Home, Page 166 - #5.

11:25 "I am the resurrection, and the life," LESSON: 148—RESURRECTION - ASCENSION—Overcoming & Returning Home, Page 166 - #6.

11:42 "I knew that thou hearest me always," LESSON: 53 (Student's Story)—DISCIPLESHIP—Accepting the Hand of Jesus, Page 69 - #5.

11:43-44 "he cried with a loud voice, Lazarus, come forth," LESSON: 102—LAZARUS RISING—Rising Stored Energy, Page 123 - #1.

12:32 "If I be lifted up from the earth, will draw all *men* unto me," LESSON: 27 (Student's Story)—BODY—Temple - Mode of Transportation, Page 42 - #8 & LESSON: 85—HOLY SPIRIT, Page 106 - #7 & LESSON: 115—"NO."—Guardian and Protector, Page 136 - #12 & LESSON: 152—SENSITIVITY—Personal Acceptance of Criticism, Page 169 - #11 & LESSON: 167—SUFFERING— Attachment, Page 184 - #12.

12:43 "For they loved the praise of men more than the praise of God," LESSON: 116 (Student's Story)—OBEDIENCE—Establishing A Balance Page 137 - #3 & LESSON: 129 (Student's Story)—PRAISE AND BLAME—

JOHN:

Are the Same, Page 148 - #7 & LESSON: 152—SENSITIVITY—Personal Acceptance of Criticism, Page 169 - #15.

13:16-17 "The servant is not greater than his lord; neither he that is sent greater than he that sent him," LESSON: 154 (Student's Story)—SERVANT I—The Christ Servant, Page 171 - #3.

13:21 "I say unto you, that one of you shall betray me," LESSON: 206—YIELDING—A Moment of Choice Surrender, Page 220 - #12.

13:35 "By this shall all *men* know you that ye are my disciples," LESSON: 31—CHARITY—God's Love Expansively Expressed, Page 48 - #4 & LESSON: 43—CONSENT—Love's Wisdom, Page 59 - #5 & LESSON: 120—PENANCE—Self-Inflicted Punishment, Page 142 - #5.

14:1 "LET not your heart be troubled," LESSON: 4—SPIRITUAL HEART CENTER—Best Kept Secret, Page 9 - #8.

14:6 "I am the way, the truth, and the life," LESSON: 1—THE SPIRITUAL WALK - JOURNEY—CHRISTIAN, Page 7 - #7 & LESSON: 13 (Student's Story)—CHRIST CENTERED PRAYER—Method, Page 24 - #14 & LESSON: 177—TRANSITION—Readiness Advance, Page 193 - #9 & LESSON: 44—CONTEMPLATIVE—Accepts the Invitation, Page 60 - #5 & LESSON: 181—TRUTH—Revealed Teaching, Page 198 - #9 & LESSON: 187 (Student's Story)—VIRGINAL CONCEPTION—Conception of Jesus, Page 204 - #12.

14:7 "If ye had known me, ye should have known my Father also," LESSON: 96 (Student's Story)—JESUS—PRE-EXISTENCE - PERSONAL - IMPERSONAL, Page 116 - **3. IMPERSONAL:** C.

14:10 "Believest thou not that I am in the Father, and the Father in me?," LESSON: 53 (Student's Story)—DISCIPLESHIP—Accepting the Hand of Jesus, Page 69 - #11 & LESSON: 87 (Student's Story)—HUMILITY—"Of myself I can do nothing," Page 108 - #5 & LESSON: 135—PRIDE—Comes Before A Fall, Page 156 - **OVERCOMING FALSE PRIDE:** A.

JOHN:

14:16 "I will pray the Father, and he shall give you another Comforter," LESSON: 85—HOLY SPIRIT—Teacher, Helper, Page 106 - #9.

14:18 "I will not leave you comfortless," LESSON: 93 (Student's Story)— INNER & OUTER—Permanence & Impermanence, Page 114 - #3.

14:19 "Yet a little while, and the world seeth me no more," CONCLUSION - A CERTAINTY, Page 230 - Paragraph 2.

14:20 "At that day ye shall know that I *am* in my Father, and ye in me, and I in you," LESSON: 1—THE SPIRITUAL WALK - JOURNEY—Christian, Page 7 - #3 & LESSON: 7—ATTACHMENT—"I, Me, My, Mine," Page 15 - #2 & LESSON: 13 (Student's Story)—CHRIST CENTERED PRAYER—Method, Page 24 - #5 & LESSON: 122—PERSECUTION - CRUCIFIXION—False Sense and Giving It Up, Page 143 - #4 & CONCLUSION - A CERTAINTY, Page 230 - Paragraph 5.

14:26 "the Comforter, *which is* the Holy Ghost, whom the Father will send in my name, he shall teach you all thing," LESSON: 44— CONTEMPLATIVE—Accepts the Invitation, Page 60 - #3 & LESSON: 61 (Student's Story)—EUCHARIST—Gift of Remembrance, Page 81 - #5 & LESSON: 85—HOLY SPIRIT—Teacher, Helper, Page 106 - #6 & LESSON: 122—PERSECUTION - CRUCIFIXION—False Sense and Giving It Up, Page 143 - #3 & LESSON: 181—TRUTH—Revealed Teaching, Page 198 - Definition & LESSON: 207—ZONE—Designated Area, Page 22 - #4.

14:27 "Peace I leave with you, my peace I give unto you not as the world giveth," LESSON: 158—SILENCE - OUTER & INNER—The Still Small Voice, Page 176 - #6.

15:5 "I am the vine, ye *are* the branches," LESSON: 87 (Student's Story)—HUMILITY—"Of myself I can do nothing," Page 108 - #3.

15:7 "If ye abide in me, and my words abide in you, ye shall ask what ye will, and it shall be done unto you," LESSON: 87 (Student's Story)—HUMILITY—"Of myself I can do nothing," Page 108 - #4 &

JOHN:

LESSON: 116 (Student's Story)—OBEDIENCE—Establishing A Balance, Page 137 - #4.

15:8 "Herein is my Father glorified, that ye bear much fruit; so shall ye be my disciples," LESSON: 53 (Student's Story)—DISCIPLESHIP—Accepting the Hand of Jesus, Page 69- #1.

15:13 "Greater love hath no man than this, that a man lay down his life for his friends," LESSON: 61 (Student's Story)—EUCHARIST—Gift of Remembrance, Page 81 - #1 & LESSON: 122—PERSECUTION - CRUCI-FIXION—False Sense and Giving It Up, Page 143 - **PERSECUTION:** B.

15:26 "But when the Comforter is come, whom I will send unto you from the Father, even the Spirit of truth, which proceedeth from the Father," LESSON: 73—FREE - TOTALLY—What You Are, Page 95 - #2.

16:13 "when he, the Spirit of truth, is come, he will guide you into all truth," LESSON: 181—TRUTH—Revealed Teaching, Page 198 - #2.

16:15 "All things that the Father hath are mine: therefore said I, that he shall take of mine, and shall shew *it* unto you," LESSON: 99—KINGDOM—Natural Inheritance, Page 119 - #5.

16:22 "ye now therefore have sorrow: but I will see you again and your heart shall rejoice," LESSON: 97—JOY—Inner Contentment, Page 118 - #3.

16:33 "I have overcome the world," LESSON: 60 (Student's Story)—ENOUGH IS ENOUGH!—Giving In to A Realization, Page 79 - #3 & LESSON: 18—ADVERSITY—Feelings of Wretchedness, Page 36 - #4 & LESSON 73—FREE - TOTALLY—What You Are, Page 95 - #8 & LESSON: 92—IMPERSONAL—Immortal God Being, Page 113 - #5 & LESSON 148—RESURRECTION - ASCENSION—Overcoming & Returning Home, Page 166 - #7.

17:3 "this is eternal life, that they may know thee, the only true God," LESSON: 44—CONTEMPLATIVE—Accepts the Invitation, Page 60 - #7 & LESSON: 131—PRAYING - PRAYERS—Hail Mary, Lord's Prayer, Rosary,

JOHN:

Page 150 - **LORD'S PRAYER:** L. & LESSON: 181—TRUTH—Revealed Teaching, Page 198 - #4 & LESSON: 190 (Student's Story)—VOID—Inexplicable, Page 208 - #8 & CONCLUSION - A CERTAINTY, Page 230 - Paragraph 1.

17:4 "I have glorified thee on earth: I have finished the work which thou gavest me to do," LESSON: 101—LAYERS—Three Major Layers, Page 121 - **SPIRITUAL LAYER: #2.**

17:5 "now, O Father, glorify thou me with thine own self with the glory which I had with thee before the world," LESSON: 26—BIRTH—DEATH—Imaginary Cycle, Page 41 - #7 & LESSON: 74—FREEDOM—Reality of the Christ, Page 96 - #10 & LESSON: 92—IMPERSONAL—Immortal God Being, Page 113 - Definition & LESSON: 96 (Student's Story)—JESUS-PRE-EXISTENCE-PERSONAL-IMPERSONAL, Page 116 - **1. PRE-EXISTENCE:** A. & LESSON: 101—LAYERS—Three Major Layers, Page 121 **SPIRITUAL LAYER:** #3 & LESSON: 109—MARRIAGE—Fluid Occurrence On Plane of Opposites, Page 132 - # 16.

17:16 "They are not of the world, even as I am not," LESSON: 44—CONTEMPLATIVE—Accepts the Invitation, Page 60 - #4 & LESSON: 93 (Student's Story)—INNER & OUTER—Permanence & Impermanence, Page 114 - #8 & LESSON: 166—STRANGER—Meeting Yourself, Page 18 - #9.

17:20-21 "Neither pray I for these alone, but for them also which shall believe on me through their word," LESSON: 96 (Student's Story)—JESUS—PRE-EXISTENCE - PERSONAL - IMPERSONAL, Page 116 - **3. IMPERSONAL:** A. & CONCLUSION - A CERTAINTY, Page 230 - Paragraph 6 & 7.

17:21 "That they all may be one; as thou, Father, *art* in me, and I am in thee," LESSON: 5 (Student's Story)—AWARENESS - CONSCIOUSNESS—The Changeless, Individual Expressions, Page 10 - #18.

17:22-23 "the glory which thou gavest me I have given them; that they may be one, even as we are one," LESSON: 32—CHANGE - CONVERSION—The Inevitable, Page 48 - #5.

JOHN:

17:25 "O righteous Father, the world hath not known thee, but I have known thee," LESSON: 93 (Student's Story)—INNER & OUTER—Permanence & Impermanence, Page 114 - # 5.

18:36 "My kingdom is not of this world," LESSON: 131—PRAYING - PRAYERS—Hail Mary, Lord's Prayer, and Rosary, Page 150 - **LORD'S PRAYER:** F. & LESSON: 152—SENSITIVITY—Personal Acceptance of Criticism, Page 169 - #3.

19:11 "Thou couldest have no power *at all* against me," LESSON: 111—MIND—Thinking/Memory, Feelings, Emotions, Page 133 - #7 & LESSON: 170—SYMBOLS AND RITUALS—Forms and Practices, Page 188 - #3.

19:25 "Now there stood by the cross of Jesus his mother," LESSON: 112—MOTHER MARY - SPIRIT OF MARY—Patient Guidance, Page 134 - #3.

19:34 "one of the soldiers with a spear pierced his side," LESSON: 125—PIERCING—Attempts to Penetrate the Christ Amour, Page 145 - #7.

20:17 "Touch me not; for I am not yet ascended to my Father," LESSON: 85—HOLY SPIRIT—Teacher, Helper, Page 106 - #12.

20:21-22 "as my Father hath sent me, even so send I you," LESSON: 28—BREATH—God's Life Force, Page 45 - #5.

21:16-17 "Lord thou knowest all things; thou knowest that I love thee. Jesus saith unto him, Feed my sheep," LESSON: 42—CONSCIOUSNESS - RECOGNITION—Knowing Differences, Page 58 - #11.

*   *   *

ACTS:

2:4 "They were all filled with the Holy Ghost Holy Ghost and began to speak in other tongues," LESSON: 121—PENTECOST—Holy Spirit Reality, Page 142 - #2.

2:38-39 'Repent, and be baptized every one of you in the name of Jesus Christ," LESSON: 24—BAPTISM—Water and Spirit Invitation, Page 40 - #5.

5:16 "There came also a multitude *out* of the cities round about unto Jerusalem, bringing sick folks, and them," LESSON: 81—HEALING—Truth Revealed, Page 103 - #2.

5:29 "We ought obey God rather than men," LESSON: 116 (Student's Story)—OBEDIENCE—Establishing A Balance, Page 137 - #2.

9:6 "Lord what wilt thou have me do," LESSON: 182—TRYING—Built in Failure, Page 199 - #6.

15:8-9 "God, which knoweth the hearts, bare them witness, giving them the Holy Ghost," LESSON: 98—JUDGING—To Bring into Question, Page 119 - #6.

15:9 "put no difference between us and them, purifying their hearts by faith," LESSON: 13 (Student's Story)—CHRIST CENTERED PRAYER—Method, Page 24 - #20.

ACTS:

17:27 "That they should seek the Lord, if haply they might feel after him, and find him," LESSON: 7—ATTACHMENT—"I, Me, My, Mine," Page 15 - #1.

17:28 "For in him we live, and move, and have our being; as certain also of your own poets," LESSON: 7 (Student's Story)—ATTACHMENT— "I, Me, My, Mine," Page 15 - Definition & LESSON 40—CONFIDENCE, Page 57 - #1 & LESSON: 96—JESUS—PRE-EXISTENCE - PERSONAL - IMPERSONAL, Page 116 - **PRE-EXISTENCE:** C.

20:1 "after the uproar was ceased, Paul called unto *him* the disciples, and embraced *them,*" LESSON: 86—HUGS—Acceptance and Parting Embrace, Page 107 - #6.

24:15 "have hope toward God, which they themselves also allow, that there shall be a resurrection of the dead," LESSON: 48— RESURRECTION - ASCENSION—Overcoming & Returning Home, Page 166 - #4.

*   *   *

ROMANS:

1:17 "For therein is the righteousness of God revealed from faith to faith: as it is written, The just shall live by faith," LESSON: 66—FAITH—The Kingdom of God, Page 87 - #7.

2:3 "thinkest thou this, O man, that judgest them which do such things, and doest the same, that thou shalt escape the judgment of God," LESSON: 98—JUDGING—To Bring into Question, Page 119 - #7.

5:5 "hope maketh not ashamed; because the love of God is shed abroad in our hearts by the Holy Ghost which is given unto us," LESSON: 131—PRAYING - PRAYERS—Hail Mary, Lord's Prayer, Rosary, Page 150 - **THE LORD'S PRAYER:** C.

5:10-11 "FOR IF, WHEN we were enemies, we were reconciled to God by the death of his Son, much more, being reconciled, we shall be saved by his life," LESSON: 141 (Student's Story)—RECONCILIATION - ATONE-MENT - SALVATION—Acceptance, Page 159 - Definition.

6:23 "For the wages of sin *is* death; but the gift of God *is* eternal life through Jesus Christ our Lord," LESSON: 76—GIFTS—Necessary Assistance, Page 98 - **GIFTS TO AWAKEN YOU:** A.

7:11 "For sin, taking occasion by the commandment, deceived me, and by it slew *me,*" LESSON: 58—EGO—Bloated False Sense of Humility, Page 78 - #8.

7:25 "thank God through Jesus Christ our Lord. So then with the mind I myself serve the law of God; but with the flesh the law of sin," LESSON:

ROMANS:

36—COMPARING—Paper Credentials, Page 53 - #7 & LESSON: 20—ANALYZING—Mind/Intellect's Nature, Page 37 - #5 & LESSON: 111—MIND—Thinking, Memory, Feelings, and Emotions, Page 133 - #12.

8:1-2 "*There is* therefore now no condemnation to them which are in Christ Jesus, who walk not after the flesh, but after the Spirit," LESSON 20—ANALYZING—Mind/Intellect's Nature, Page 37 - #7 & LESSON: 186—VANITY—Unnecessary Attention to the Physical Appearance, Page 203 - #6.

8:9 "ye are not in the flesh, but in the Spirit, if so be that the Spirit of God dwell in you," LESSON: 123—PERSON—A Separative False Sense of Reality, Page 144 - #1.

8:11 "if the Spirit of him that raised up Jesus from the dead dwell in you, he that raised up Christ from the dead shall also quicken your," LESSON: 73—FREE - TOTALLY—What You Are, Page 95 - #1.

8:14 "For as many as are led by the Spirit of God, they are the sons of God," LESSON: 91—IMPATIENCE—Pressing Against the Gates of Heaven, Page 112 - #7.

8:16-17 "The Spirit itself beareth witness with our spirit, that we are the children of God," LESSON: 191 (Student's Story)—VULNERABLE—False Sense of Separation, Page 209 - #10.

8:18 "For I reckon that the sufferings of this present time *are* not worthy *to be compared* with the glory which shall be revealed in us," LESSON: 22—ANOINTING—Invested Power, Page 39 - #3.

8:25 "But if we hope for that we see not, *then* do we with patience wait for *it*," LESSON: 119—PATIENCE—Staying in Place, Page 141 - #3.

9:32 "Wherefore? Because *they sought it* not by faith, but as it were by the works of the law. For they stumbled at that stumbling stone," LESSON: 66—FAITH—The Kingdom of God, Page 87 - #1.

ROMANS:

10:10 "For with the heart man believeth unto righteousness; and with the mouth confession is made unto salvation," LESSON: 4—SPIRITUAL HEART CENTER—Best Kept Secret, Page 9 - #4.

13:1 "I *am* the first, and I *am* the last; and beside me *there is* no god," LESSON: 170—SYMBOLS AND RITUALS—Forms and Practices, Page 188 - #4.

13:10 "Love worketh no ill to his neighbour," LESSON: 100—LANGUAGE—Expressions of Communication - Spoken Word, Page 120 - **3. UNIVERSAL LANGUAGE:** D.

13:12 "The night is far spent, the day is at hand let us therefore cast off the works of darkness, and let us put on the armour of light," LESSON: 40—CONFIDENCE—Total Trust, Page 57- #8.

13:14 "put ye on the Lord Jesus Christ, and make not provision for the flesh to *fulfill* the lusts *thereof,*" LESSON: 26—BIRTH - DEATH—Imaginary Cycle, Page 41 - #3.

14:10 "why dost thou judge thy brother? Or why dost thou set at nought thy brother?," LESSON: 120—PENANCE - Self-Inflicted Punishment, Page 142 - Definition.

14:17-18 "the kingdom of God is not meat and drink; but righteousness, and peace, and joy in the Holy Ghost," LESSON: 17—ACCEPTANCE—Accepting the Acceptance of the Christ, Page 35 - #7.

14:19 "Let us therefore follow after the things which make for peace, and things wherewith one may edify another," LESSON: 39—CONCENTRATION—One Pointedness, Page 55 - #7.

*   *   *

I. CORINTHIANS:

2:9 "Eye hath not seen, nor ear heard neither have entered into the heart of man the things which God hath prepared for them that love him," LESSON: 59 (Student's Story)—ENLIGHTENMENT—After-Effect, Page 78 - **STUDENT'S STORY:** Paragraph 1 & LESSON: 64 (Student's Story)—EXPECTATIONS—Anticipations - Disappointments, Page 84 - 16.

2:12 "Now we have received, not the spirit of the world, but the Spirit which is of God," LESSON: 78—GRATITUDE—Standing on Holy Ground, Page 99 - #6.

3:16 "Know ye not that ye are the temple of God, and *that* the Spirit of God dwelleth in you?," LESSON: 72—FOOD—Medicine for the Body, Page 93 - #12 & LESSON: 27 (Student's Story)—BODY—Temple - Mode of Transportation, Page 42 - #5 & LESSON: 101—LAYERS—Three Major Layers, Page 121 - **PHYSICAL SENSE LAYER:** E.

6:14 "God hath both raised the Lord, and will also raise up us by his own power," LESSON: 148—RESURRECTION - ASCENSION—Overcoming & Returning Home, Page166 - #10.

6:19-20 "ye are not your own? For ye are bought with a price: therefore glorify God," LESSON: 72—FOOD—Medicine For the Body, Page 93 - **SUGGESTIONS:** C. & LESSON: 186—VANITY—Unnecessary Attention to the Physical Appearance, Page 203 - #10.

7:7-9 "I would that all men were even as I myself. But every man hath his proper gift of God, one after this manner, and another after that," LESSON

I. CORINTHIANS:

30 (Student's Story)—CELIBACY—Abstention of Sexual Energy, Page 46 - #2.

8:2 "if any man think that he knoweth any thing, he knoweth nothing yet as he ought to know," LESSON: 171—TEACHERS—Three Types, Page 188 - #2.

9:14 "the Lord ordained that they which preach the gospel should live of the gospel," LESSON:179 (Student's Story)—TRUST II: TRUST IN A CHRIST CENTERED TEACHER, Page 195 - #5.

12:9 "To another faith by same Spirit; to another the gifts of healing," LESSON: 22—ANOINTING—Invested Power, Page 39 - #1 & LESSON: 81—HEALING—Truth Revealed, Page 103 - #7.

12:10 "To another the working of miracles; to another prophecy," LESSON: 52—DISCERNMENT—Clarity of Perception, Page 69 - #6.

12:11 "all these worketh that one and the selfsame Spirit," LESSON: 124—PERSONALITY—Distinctive Qualities, Page 144 - #4.

13:2 "and though I have all faith, so that I could remove mountains, and have not charity, I am nothing," LESSON: 31—CHARITY—God's Love Expansively Expressed, Page 48 - #2.

13:3 "though I give my body to be burned, and not charity, it profiteth me nothing," LESSON: 31—CHARITY—God's Love Expansively Expressed, Page 48 - #1.

13:4-7 "Charity suffereth long, *and* is kind; charity envieth not; charity vaunteth not, is not puffed up," LESSON: 31—CHARITY—God's Love Expansively Expressed, Page 48 - #7.

13:9-10 "For we know in part, and we prophesy in part," LESSON: 103 (Student's Story)—LESSONS - MISTAKES & ERRORS—Manifested Guidance, Page 125 - **LESSONS:** #9.

I. CORINTHIANS:

13:11-12 "now we see through a glass, darkly," LESSON 103 (Student's Story)—LESSONS - MISTAKES - ERRORS—Manifested Guidance, Page 125 - **MISTAKES—ERRORS: #1.**

13:13 "now abideth faith, hope, charity; these three; but the greatest of these *is* charity," LESSON 31—CHARITY—God's Love expansively Expressed, Page 48 - #8.

15:12-14 "And if Christ be not risen, then *is* our preaching vain, and your faith *is* also vain," LESSON: 148—RESURRECTION - ASCENSION—Overcoming & Returning Home, Page 166 - #9.

15:36 "*Thou* fool, that which thou sowest is not quickened, except it die," LESSON: 5 (Student's Story)—AWARENESS - CONSCIOUSNESS—The Changeless, Individual Expressions, Page 10 - #8.

15:42-43 "So also *is* the resurrection of the dead. sown in corruption; raised in incorruption," LESSON: 148—RESURRECTION - ASCENSION—Overcoming & Returning Home, Page 166 - #8.

15:51 "Behold, I shew you a mystery; We shall not all sleep, but we shall all be changed," LESSON: 70—FLEXIBILITY—Freedom to Adjust, Page 92 - #10.

*   *   *

II. CORINTHIANS:

5:7 "For we walk by faith, not by sight," LESSON: 193—WALKING ALONE—Feeling Abandon by God, Page 211 - #3.

5:17 "If any man *be* in Christ, *he is* a new creature," LESSON: 55 (Student's Story)—DRAMA—Hyper-Response/Reaction, Page 73 - #8 & LESSON: 152—SENSITIVITY—Personal Acceptance of Criticism, Page 169 - #4.

5:21 "For he hath made him *to be* in sin for us, who knew no sin," LESSON: 85—HOLY SPIRIT—Teacher, Helper, Page 106 - #2.

6:16 "For ye are the living temple of God," LESSON: 85—HOLY SPIRIT—Teacher, Helper, Page 106 - #14.

6:17 "Wherefore come out from among them, and be ye separate," LESSON: 179 (Student's Story)—TRUST II—Teacher's Responsibility, Page 195 - #1.

6:18 "And will be a Father unto you, and ye shall be my sons and daughters, saith the Lord Almighty," LESSON: 85—HOLY SPIRIT—Teacher, Helper, Page 106 - #14.

8:11 "perform the doing *of it*; as *there was* a readiness to will, so *there may be* a performance also out of that which ye have," LESSON: 177—TRANSITION—Readiness Advance, 193 - #6.

9:6 "He which soweth sparingly shall reap also sparingly" LESSON: 168 (Student's Story)—SUPPLY—Spiritual Principle, Page 185 - #18.

II. CORINTHIANS:

12:9 "My grace is sufficient for thee: for my strength is made perfect in weakness," LESSON: 77—GRACE—Light of Awareness, Page 99 - #3.

13:8 "For we can do nothing against the truth, but for the truth," LESSON: 181—TRUTH—Revealed Teaching, Page 198 - #8.

21:22 "Now he which stablisheth us with you in Christ, and hath anointed us, *is* God," LESSON: 4—SPIRITUAL HEART CENTER—Best Kept Secret, Page 9 - #1.

*   *   *

GALATIANS:

2:20 "I am crucified with Christ: nevertheless I live; yet not I, but Christ liveth in me," LESSON: 67 (Student's Story)—FAITHFULNESS—Standing Firm, Page 87 - #10.

3:3 "Are ye so foolish? having begun in the Spirit, are ye now made perfect by the flesh?," LESSON: 123—PERSON—A Separative False Sense of Reality, Page 144 - #5.

3:28 "There is neither Jew nor Greek, there is neither bond nor free, there is neither male nor female: for ye are all one in Christ Jesus," LESSON: 143—REFLECTION—God's Image, Page 163 - #5.

4:6 "And because you are children, God hath sent the Spirit of his Son into our hearts, crying, Abba! Father!," LESSON: 4—SPIRITUAL HEART CENTER—Best Kept Secret, Page 9 - #2 & LESSON: 177—TRANSITION—Readiness Advance, Page 193 - #8.

5:4 "whosoever of you are justified by the law; ye are fallen from grace," LESSON: 68—FALL - GRAND FALL—A Descent and Starting Over, Page 89 - **SIGNS OF A POSSIBLE FALL: A.**

6:7 "Be not deceived; God is not mocked: for whatsoever a man soweth, that shall he also reap," LESSON: 72—FOOD—Medicine for the Body, Page 93 - **SUGGESTIONS: D.**

GALATIANS:

6:8 "For he that soweth to his flesh shall of the flesh reap corruption," LESSON: 43—CONSENT—Love's Wisdom, Page 59 - #8 & LESSON: 123—PERSON—A Separative False Sense of Reality, Page 144 - #6.

*   *   *

EPHESIANS:

1:6 "To the praise of the glory of his grace, wherein he hath made us accepted in the beloved," LESSON: 17—ACCEPTANCE—Accepting the Acceptance of the Christ, Page 35 - #4 & LESSON: 25—BELOVED—The One in the Many, Page 41 - #10.

2:5 "Even when we were dead in sins, hath quickened us together with Christ, (by grace ye are saved)," LESSON: 77—GRACE - Light of Awareness, Page 99 - #4.

2:18 "For through him both of us have access in one Spirit unto the Father," LESSON: 1—THE SPIRITUAL WALK - JOURNEY—Christian, Page 7 - #8 & LESSON: 13 (Student's Story)—CHRIST CENTERED PRAYER Method, Page 24 - #1 & LESSON: 197—"WHY, GOD?"—"Why, You?" Page 214 - #11 & CONCLUSION - A CERTAINTY, Page 230 - Paragraph 4.

2:19 "Now therefore ye are no more strangers and foreigners, but fellow citizens with the saints, and of the household of God," LESSON: 166—STRANGER—Meeting Yourself, Page 183 - #6.

3:17-19 "That Christ may dwell in your hearts through faith," LESSON: 107—LOVE-GOD's—God's Nature, Page 130 - #11 & LESSON: 20—ANALYZING—Mind/Intellect's Nature, Page 37 - #2.

4:4-6 "*There is* one body, and one Spirit," LESSON: 5 (Student's Story)—AWARENESS - CONSCIOUSNESS—The Changeless, Individual Expressions, Page 10 - #13.

EPHESIANS:

4:9-10 "He that descended is the same also that ascended up far above all heavens," LESSON: 148—RESURRECTION - ASCENSION— Overcoming & Returning Home, Page 166 - **ASCENSION:** #3.

4:22-24 "put off concerning the former conversation the old man, which is corrupt according to the deceitful lusts; be renewed in the spirit of your mind; And that ye put on the new man," LESSON: 124—PERSONALITY— Distinctive Qualities, Page 144 - #7.

5:14 "Awake thou that sleepest, and arise from the dead, and Christ shall give thee light," LESSON: 26—BIRTH - DEATH—Imaginary Cycle, Page 41 - #5 & LESSON: 1—THE SPIRITUAL WALK - JOURNEY—Christian, Page 7 - #5 & LESSON: 103—LESSONS - MISTAKES & ERRORS— Manifested Guidance, Page 125 - **MISTAKES & ERRORS:** #2 & LESSON: 192—WAKING UP—Returning Home, Page 210 - #10.

6:6 "Not with eye service, as men pleasers; but as the servants of Christ, doing the will of God from the heart," LESSON: 206—YIELDING—A Moment of Choice Surrender, Page 220 - #13.

*   *   *

PHILIPPIANS:

2:5 "Let this mind be in you which was also in Christ Jesus," LESSON: 5 (Student's Story)—AWARENESS - CONSCIOUSNESS—The Changeless, Individual Expressions, Page10 - #21 & LESSON: 20 (Student's Story)—ANALYZING—Mind/Intellect's Nature, Page 37 - #8 & LESSON: 124—PERSONALITY—Distinctive Qualities, Page 44 - #6 & LESSON: 50 (Student's Story)—DETACHMENT—Free from Suffering, Page 66 - #8 & LESSON: 94—INSIGHTS AND REALIZATION—Intellectual & Beyond, Page 115 - #2.

4:7 "And the peace of God, which passeth all understanding, shall keep your hearts and minds through Christ Jesus," LESSON: 8—ATTRACTION— Manifestations of Vibrating Energy, Page 17 - #16 & LESSON: 97—JOY— Inner Contentment, Page 118 - #4 & LESSON: 158—SILENCE - OUTER & INNER—The Still Small Voice, Page 176 - **THE INNER VOICE**: #5 & LESSON: 174—THOUGHTS - EMOTIONS - FEELING—Rising Vibrating Energy, Page 191 - #10.

*   *   *

COLOSSIANS:

2:10 "And ye are complete in him, which is the head of all principality and power," LESSON: 20—ANALYZING—Mind/Intellect's Nature, Page 37 - #4.

3:14 "above all these things *put on* charity, which is the bond of perfectness," LESSON: 31—CHARITY—God's Love Expansively Expressed, Page 48 - #5.

1:27 "To whom God would make known what *is* the riches of the glory of this mystery among the Gentiles; which is Christ in you, the hope of glory" LESSON: 83—HOPE—Fresh Water, Page 105 - #6.

*   *   *

I. THESSALONIANS:

5:6 "Therefore let us not sleep, as *do* others; but let us watch and be sober," LESSON: 161—SLEEP—The Need For Less, Page 178 - #7.

5:14 "Now we exhort you, brethren warn them that are unruly, comfort the feebleminded, support the weak, be patient toward all *men,*" LESSON: 119—PATIENCE—Staying in Place, Page 141 - #2.

* * *

I. TIMOTHY:

6:20 "keep that which is committed to thy trust, avoiding profane *and* vain babblings, and oppositions of science falsely so called," LESSON: 117—OPPOSITES—This Earth Plane, Page 139 - #4 & LESSON: 206—YIELDING—A Moment of Choice Surrender, Page 220 - #6.

*   *   *

II. TIMOTHY:

1:7 "God hath not given us the spirit of fear; but of power, and of love, and of a sound mind," LESSON: 191 (Student's Story)—VULNERABLE—False Sense of Separation, Page 209 - #1.

2:7 "Consider what I say; and the Lord give thee understanding in all things," LESSON: 94—INSIGHTS AND REALIZATION—Intellectual & Beyond, Page 115 - #4.

*   *   *

HEBREWS:

3:14-15 "Today if ye will hear his voice, harden not your hearts, as in the provocation," LESSON: 40—CONFIDENCE—Total Trust, Page 57 - #6.

5:8 "Though he were a Son, yet learned obedience by the things which he suffered," LESSON: 103—LESSONS - MISTAKES & ERRORS—Manifested Guidance, Page 125 - #3.

5:12 "for the time ye ought to be teachers, ye have need that one teach you again which *be* the first principles of the Oracles of God," LESSON: 103—LESSONS - MISTAKES & ERRORS—Manifested Guidance, Page 125 - #8.

9:14 "purge your conscience from dead works to service the living God," LESSON: 118—OVERCOMING—The White Robe, Page 140 - #2.

11:1 "faith is the substance of things hoped for, the evidence of things not seen," LESSON: 66—FAITH—The Kingdom of God, Page 87 - Definition.

11:3 "the worlds were framed by the word of God, so that things which are seen were not made of things which do appear," LESSON: 66—FAITH—The Kingdom of God, Page 87 - #8.

11:9 "By faith he sojourned in the land of promise, as *in* a strange country, dwelling in tabernacles with Isaac and Jacob, the heirs with him of the same promise," LESSON: 166—STRANGER—Meeting Yourself, Page 183 - #2.

HEBREWS:

12:9 "shall we not much rather be in subjection unto the Father of spirits, and live?," LESSON: 73—FREE - TOTALLY—What You Are, Page 95 - #6.

12:28 "receiving a kingdom which cannot be moved, let us have grace, whereby we may serve God acceptable with reverence and godly fear," LESSON: 154 (Student's Story)—SERVANT I—The Christ Servant, Page 171 - Definition.

13:8 "Jesus Christ the same yesterday, and to day, and for ever," CONCLUSION - A CERTAINTY, Page 230 - Paragraph 3.

*   *   *

JAMES:

4:10 "Humble yourselves in the sight the Lord, and he shall lift you up," LESSON: 87 (Student's Story)—HUMILITY—"Of myself I can do nothing," Page 108 - #16.

1:4 "let patience have *her* perfect work, that ye may be perfect and entire, wanting nothing," LESSON: 119—PATIENCE—Staying in Place, Page 141 - #11.

1:5 "If any of you lack wisdom, let him ask of God, that giveth to all *men* liberally," LESSON: 200 (Student's Story)—WISDOM—Recognition, Page 216 - #4.

*　　*　　*

I. PETER:

2:21 "Christ also suffered for us, leaving us an example, that ye should follow his steps," LESSON: 2—AN INVITATION—"Come Follow Me," Page 7 - #3.

3:13 "who *is* he that will harm you, if ye be followers of that which is good?," LESSON: 147—REMORSE—Deep Sorrow, Page 165 - #4.

4:8 "for charity shall cover the multitude of sins," LESSON: 31—CHARITY—God's Love Expansively Expressed, Page 48 - #6.

5:6 "Humble yourselves therefore under the mighty hand of God, that he may exalt you in due time," LESSON: 87 (Student's Story)—HUMILITY—"What can I of myself do?," Page 108 - Definition.

* * *

II. PETER:

1:2 "Grace and peace be multiplied unto you through the knowledge of God, and of Jesus our Lord," LESSON: 114—NEGATIVITY—Destructive Conditioning, Page 136 - #3.

1:10-11 "give diligence to make your calling an election sure: for if ye do these things, ye shall never fall," LESSON: 68—FALL - GRAND FALL—A Descent and Starting Over, Page 89 - #7.

3:9 "that all should come to repentance," LESSON: 147—REMORSE—Deep Sorrow, Page 165 - #3.

*   *   *

I. JOHN:

1:14 "the Word was made flesh, and dwelt among us" LESSON: 100—LANGUAGE—Expressions of Communication, Page 120 - **SPOKEN WORD:** #3.

2:15 "If any man love the world, the love of the Father is not in him," LESSON: 67 (Student Story)—FAITHFULNESS—Standing Firm, Page 87 - #7.

2:16 "all that is in the world, the lust of the flesh, and the lust of the eyes, and the pride of life, is not of the Father, but is of the world," LESSON: 53 (Student's Story)—DISCIPLESHIP—Accepting the Hand of Jesus, Page 69 - #8.

2:17 "the world passeth away, and the lust thereof: but he that doeth the will of God abideth for ever," LESSON: 43—CONSENT—Love's Wisdom, Page 59 - #6.

3:1 "the world knoweth us not, because it knew him not," LESSON: 94—INSIGHTS AND REALIZATION—Intellectual & Beyond, Page 115 - #3 & LESSON: 107—LOVE-GOD's—God's Nature, Page 130 - #1 & LESSON: 197—"WHY, GOD?"—"Why, You?" Page 214 - #14.

3:2 "Beloved, now are we the sons of God," LESSON: 25—BELOVED—The One in the Many, Page 41 - #7.

3:3 "every man that hath this hope in him purifieth himself, even as he is pure," LESSON: 83—HOPE—Fresh Water, Page 105 - #2.

I. JOHN:

3:9 "Whosoever is born of God doth not commit sin; for his seed remaineth in him: and he cannot sin, because he is born of God," LESSON: 159—SIN—False Concept, Page 177 - #2.

3:18-19 "let us not love in word neither in tongue; but in deed and in truth," LESSON: 181—TRUTH—Revealed Teaching, Page 198 - #6 & LESSON: 142—REFERENCE—What Others Say and What You Know, Page 162 - #6.

4:4 "greater is he that is in you, than he that is in the world," LESSON: 53 (Student's Story)—DISCIPLESHIP—Accepting the Hand of Jesus, Page 69 - #9 & LESSON 73—FREE - TOTALLY—What You Are, Page 95 - #12 & LESSON: 131—PRAYING - PRAYERS—Hail Mary, Lord's Prayer, Rosary, Page 150 - **LORD'S PRAYER: K**.

4:5-6 "we are of God: he that knoweth God heareth us," LESSON: 7 ATTACHMENT—"I, ME, MY, MINE," Page 15 - #20 & LESSON: 36—COMPARING—Paper Credentials, Page 53 - #8.

4:8 "He that loveth not knoweth not God; for God is love," LESSON: 11—PURIFICATION PROCESS—Spiritual House Cleaning, Page 22 - **PURIFIERS: A**.

4:11 "Beloved, if God so loved us, we ought also to love one another," LESSON: 25—BELOVED—The One in the Many, Page 41 - #8.

4:16 "God is love; and he that dwelleth in love dwelleth in God and God in him," LESSON 100—LANGUAGE—Expressions of Communication, Page 120 - **3. UNIVERSAL LANGUAGE: B**. & LESSON: 169—SURRENDER—Being at Home, Page 187 - #7.

4:18 "perfect love casteth out fear," LESSON: 69—FEAR—Stumbling Block, Page 91 - #16.

4:21 "this commandment have we from him, That he who loveth God love his brother also," LESSON: 100—LANGUAGE—Expressions of Communication. Spoken Word, Page 120 - **3. UNIVERSAL LANGUAGE: E**.

I. JOHN:

5:4-5 "whatsoever is born of God overcometh the world," LESSON: 18—ADVERSITY—Feelings of Wretchedness, Page 36 - #5 & LESSON: 118—OVERCOMING—The White Robe, Page 140 - #4.

5:7 "there are three that bear record in heaven, the Father, the Word, and the Holy Ghost: and these three are one," LESSON: 85—HOLY SPIRIT—Teacher, Helper, Page 106 - #8.

5:21 "keep yourselves from idols," LESSON: 8—ATTRACTION— Manifestations of Vibrating Energy, Page 17 - #4.

*   *   *

II. JOHN:

5:14 "this is the confidence that we have in him, if we ask any thing according to his will he heareth us," LESSON: 125—PIERCING—Attempts to Penetrate the Christ Amour, 145 - #6.

* * *

REVELATIONS:

1:8 "I am Alpha and Omega, the beginning and the ending, saith the Lord," LESSON: 27 (Student's Story)—BODY—Temple - Mode of Transportation, Page 42 - #2.

2:7 "To him that overcometh will I give to eat of the tree of life, which is in the midst of the paradise of God," LESSON: 118—OVERCOMING—The White Robe, Page 140 - #5.

3:3 "If therefore thou shalt not watch, I will come on thee as a thief, and thou shalt not know what hour I will come upon thee," LESSON: 18—Adversity—Feelings of Wretchedness, Page 36 - #7.

3:5 "He that overcometh, the same shall be clothed in white raiment" LESSON: 92—IMPERSONAL—Immortal God Being, Page 113 - #7 & LESSON: 118—OVERCOMING—The White Robe, Page 140 - #8 & LESSON: 186—VANITY—Unnecessary Attention to the Physical Appearance, Page 203 - #12.

3:11 "Behold, I come quickly: hold that fast which thou hast, that no man take thy crown," LESSON: 142—REFERENCE—What Others Say and What You Know, Page 162 - #3.

3:12 "Him that overcometh will I make a pillar in the temple of my God, and he shall go no more out and I will write upon him the name of my God," LESSON: 18—ADVERSITY—Feelings of Wretchedness, Page 36 - #6 & LESSON: 26—BIRTH - DEATH—Imaginary Cycle, Page 41 - #12 & LESSON: 92—IMPERSONAL—Immortal God Being, Page 113 - #8

REVELATIONS:

& LESSON: 186—VANITY—Unnecessary Attention to the Physical Appearance, Page 203 - #8.

3:20 "I stand at the door: if any man hear my voice, and open the door, I will come in to him," LESSON: 13 (Student's Story)—CHRIST CENTERED PRAYER—Method, Page 24 - #17 & LESSON: 23—AVOIDANCE— Turning Away, Page 39 - #6 & CONCLUSION - A CERTAINTY, Page 230 - Paragraph 9.

3:21 "him that overcometh will I grant to sit with me in my throne, even as I also overcame, and am set down with my Father in his throne," LESSON: 118—OVERCOMING—The White Robe, Page 140 - #7.

4:1-24 "immediately I was in the spirit: and, behold, a throne was set in heaven, and *one* sat on the throne," LESSON: 63—EXPANSIVE - CONSCIOUSNESS— Beyond Body Sense, Page 82 - #4.

7:13-14 "these are they which came out of great tribulation, and have washed their robes, and made them white in the blood of the Lamb," LESSON: 118—OVERCOMING—The White Robe, Page 140 - #1.

21:4 "God shall wipe away all tears from their eyes; and there shall be no more death, neither sorrow, nor crying," LESSON: 79 (Student's Story)—GRIEF—Gut Wrenching Emotional Pain, Page 101 - #16.

21:5 "he that sat upon the throne said, behold, I make all things new," LESSON: 78—GRATITUDE—Standing on Holy Ground, Page 99 - #8 & LESSON: 32—CHANGE - CONVERSION—The Inevitable, Page 48 - #12 & LESSON: 163—SOUL PAIN—Dark Days and Darker Nights, Page 180 - #10.

21:10 "he carried me away in the spirit to a great and high mountain, and shewed me that great city, the holy Jerusalem," LESSON: 63— EXPANSIVE - CONSCIOUSNESS—Beyond Body Sense, Page 82 - #3.

*   *   *

OLD TESTAMENT

(KING JAMES VERSION)

GENESIS:

1:2-3 "The Spirit of God moved upon the face of the waters. And God said, Let there be light: and there was light," LESSON: 47—CREATION—In the Light of Awareness, Page 62 - #3.

1:28 "Be fruitful and multiply," LESSON: 47—CREATION—In the Light of Awareness, Page 62 - #5.

1:26 "And God said, Let us make man in our image, after our likeness," LESSON: 27 (Student's Story)—BODY—Temple - Mode of Transportation, Page 42 - #1.

1:27 "in the image of God created he him; male and female created he them," LESSON: 47—CREATION—In the Light of Awareness, Page 62 - #4 & LESSON: 162—SOUL—Breath of God, Page 179 - #5.

2:7 "God formed man *of* the dust of the ground, and breathed into his nostrils the breath of life; and man became a living soul," LESSON: 28—BREATH—God's Life Force, Page 45 - #3 & LESSON: 93 (Student's Story)—INNER & OUTER—Permanence & Impermanence, Page 114 - #10.

2:17 "for in the day that thou eatest thereof thou shalt surely die," LESSON: 117—OPPOSITES—This Earth Plane, Page 139 - #3.

6:5 "God saw that the wickedness of man *was* great in the earth and *that* every imagination of the thoughts of his heart *was* evil continually," LESSON: 26—BIRTH - DEATH—Imaginary Cycle, Page 41 - #4.

*   *   *

EXODUS:

3:5 "for the place whereon thou standest *is* holy ground," LESSON: 78—GRATITUDE—Standing on Holy Ground, Page 99 - Definition.

3:14 "I AM THAT I AM," LESSON: 64 (Student's Story)—EXPECTA-TIONS—Anticipations - Disappointments, Page 84 - #13 & LESSON: 87—HUMILITY (Student's Story)—"Of myself I can do nothing," Page 108 - #19.

3:14-15 "I AM THAT I AM . . . this is my name forever," LESSON: 32—CHANGE - CONVERSION—The Inevitable, Page 48 - #7.

20:3 "Thou shalt have no other gods before me: LESSON: 27 (Student's Story) BODY—Temple—Mode of Transportation, Page 42 - #16.

20:4 "thou shalt not make unto thee any graven image, or any likeness *of any thing,*" LESSON: 27 (Student's Story) BODY—Temple—Mode of Transportation, Page 42 - #15.

*   *   *

LEVITICUS:

19:18 "thou shalt love thy neighour as thyself: I *am* the LORD," LESSON: 31—CHARITY—God's Love Expansively Expressed, Page 48 - Definition.

* * *

DEUTERONOMY I:

6:4 "The LORD our God *is* one LORD," LESSON: 117—OPPOSITES—This Earth Plane, Page 139 - #1.

32:4 "He *is* the Rock, his work *is* perfect: for all his ways *are* judgment," LESSON: 181—TRUTH—Revealed Teaching, Page 198 - #1.

33:12 "The beloved of the LORD shall dwell in safety by him; *and the LORD* shall dwell in safety by him," LESSON: 25—BELOVED—The One in the Many, Page 41 - #6.

33:27 "The eternal God *is thy* refuge," LESSON: 76—GIFTS—Necessary Assistance, Page - 98 - **GIFTS TO AWAKEN YOU:** F.

*　*　*

JOSHUA:

24:15 "choose you this day whom ye will serve," LESSON: 33 (Student's Story)—CHOICES & DECISIONS—Selection Carry Through, Page 50 - #12 & LESSON: 46—COURAGE—Being Brave on a Spiritual Walk, Page 62 - #2.

*   *   *

I. SAMUEL:

3:4 "Here *am* I," LESSON: 13 (Student's Story)—CHRIST CENTERED PRAYER—Method, Page 24 - #19.

3:9 "if he call thee, that thou shalt say, Speak LORD; for thy servant heareth," LESSON: 104—LISTENING—Guidance from the Spiritual Heart Center, Page 126 - #4 & LESSON: 154 (Student's Story)—SERVANT I—The Christ Servant, Page 171 - #1.

3:10 "Speak for thy servant hearth," LESSON: 76—GIFTS—Necessary Assistance, Page 98 - **GIFTS TO AWAKEN YOU: E.**

16:6-7 "the *LORD seeth* not as a man seeth; for man looketh on the outward appearance, but the LORD looketh on the heart," LESSON: 185 (Student's Story)—VALUING & APPRECIATING—What You Realize, Page 201 - #11.

16:7 "the *LORD seeth* not as a man seeth," LESSON: 70—FLEXIBILITY— Freedom to Adjust, 92 - #4.

*　　*　　*

II. SAMUEL:

22:33 "God *is* my strength *and* power: he maketh my way perfect," LESSON: 3—STRAIGHT GATE AND NARROW WAY—The Direct Path, Page 8 - #10.

* * *

I. KINGS:

8:12 "The LORD said that he would dwell in the thick darkness," LESSON: 163—SOUL PAIN—Dark Days and Darker Nights, Page 180 - #12.

19:12 "and after the fire a still small voice," LESSON: 158—SILENCE - OUTER & INNER—The Still Small Voice, Page 176 - **INNER SILENCE:** #1.

*   *   *

II. CHRONICLES:

20:15 "for the battle *is* not yours but God's," LESSON: 116 (Student's Story)—OBEDIENCE—Establishing A Balance, Page137 - #16 & LESSON: 158—SILENCE - OUTER & INNER—The Still Small Voice, Page 176 - **OUTER:** #2.

*   *   *

NEHEMIAH:

8:10 "for the joy of the LORD is your strength," LESSON: 97—JOY—Inner Contentment, Page 118 - #5.

*   *   *

JOB:

19:26 "yet in my flesh shall I see God," LESSON: 27 (Student's Story)—BODY—Temple - Mode of Transportation, Page 42 - #6.

23:14 "For he performeth the thing that is appointed for me," LESSON: 54—DOUBTS—Obstacles and Hindrances, Page 71 - #14.

26:7 "He stretcheth out the north over the empty place *and* hangeth the earth upon nothing," LESSON: 96 (Student's Story)—JESUS - PRE-EXISTENCE - PERSONAL - IMPERSONAL, Page 116 - **I PRE-EXISTENCE: G.**

28:17-18 "for the price of wisdom *is* above rubies," LESSON: 200 (Student's Story)—WISDOM—Recognition, Page 216 - #12.

32:8 "*there is* a spirit in man: and the inspiration of the Almighty giveth them understanding," LESSON: 85—HOLY SPIRIT—Teacher, Helper, Page 106 - Definition & LESSON: 95—INSPIRATION—Colors the Black and White Pictures of Life, Page 116 - #1.

*   *   *

PSALMS:

2:1 "Why do the heathen rage, and the people imagine a vain thing?," LESSON: 8—ATTRACTION—Manifestations of Vibrating Energy, Page 17 - #8.

16:11 "Thou wilt shew me the path of life: in thy presence *is* fulness of joy; at thy right hand *there are* pleasures for evermore," LESSON: 32—CHANGE - CONVERSION—The Inevitable, Page 48 - #11 & LESSON: 97—JOY—Inner Contentment, Page 118 - #1 & LESSON: 116 (Student's Story)—OBEDIENCE—Establishing A Balance, Page 137 - #18 & LESSON: 183—TWO WORLDS, Page 200 - #9.

17:15 "As for me, I will behold thy face in righteousness: I shall be satisfied, when I awake, with thy likeness," LESSON: 38—COMPLACENCY—Satisfied With the Distance Traveled, Page 55 - #2.

18:28 "For thou wilt light my candle: the LORD my God will enlighten my darkness," LESSON: 18—ADVERSITY—Feelings of Wretchedness, Page 36 - #10.

19:14 "Let the words of my mouth, and the meditation of my heart, be acceptable in thy sight, O LORD, my strength, and my redeemer," LESSON 17—ACCEPTANCE—Accepting the Acceptance of the Christ, Page 35 - #2 & LESSON: 100—LANGUAGE—Expressions of Communication, Page 120 - Definition.

23:1 "Lord is my shepherd; I shall not want," LESSON: 168 (Student's Story)—SUPPLY—Spiritual Principle, Page 185 - #5.

23:4 "Yea, though I walk through the valley of the shadow of death, I will fear no evil: for thou *art* with me; thy rod and thy staff they comfort me," LESSON: 107—LOVE-GOD's—God's Nature, Page 130 - #5.

PSALMS:

24:3-4 "Who shall ascend into the hill of the LORD? Or who shall stand in his holy place? He that hath clean hands, and a pure heart; who hath not lifted up his soul unto vanity, nor sworn deceitfully," LESSON: 186—VANITY—Unnecessary Attention to the Physical Appearance, Page 203 - #3.

25:4 "Shew me thy ways, O LORD; teach me thy paths," LESSON: 103—LESSONS—MISTAKES & ERRORS—Manifested Guidance, Page 125 - **LESSONS**: #2.

26:1 "Judge me, O LORD; for I have walked in mine integrity: I have trusted also in the LORD; *therefore* I shall not slide," LESSON: 183—TWO WORLDS, Page 200 - **MAINTAINING A BALANCE:** G.

26:11 "But as for me, I will walk in mine integrity: redeem me, and be merciful unto me" LESSON: 183—TWO WORLDS, Page 200 - **MAINTAINING A BALANCE:** E.

27:1 "The LORD *is* my light and my salvation; whom shall I fear? The LORD *is* the strength of my life; of whom shall I be afraid?," LESSON: 40—CONFIDENCE—Total Trust, Page 57 - #2 & LESSON: 152—SENSITIVITY—Personal Acceptance of Criticism, Page 169 - #16.

27:3 "Though an host should encamp against me, my heart shall not fear: though war should rise against me, in this *will* I be confident," LESSON: 40—CONFIDENCE—Total Trust, Page 57 - #5.

32:8 "I will instruct ye and teach ye in the way which thou shalt go: I will guide thee with mine eye," LESSON: 103—LESSONS—MISTAKES & ERRORS—Manifested Guidance, Page 125 - **LESSONS**: #1.

37:7 "Rest in the LORD, and wait patiently for him: fret not thyself because of him who prospereth in his way," LESSON: 91—IMPATIENCE—Pressing Against the Gates of Heaven, Page 112 - #9.

40:1 "I WAITED patiently for the LORD; and he inclined unto me, and heard my cry," LESSON: 91—IMPATIENCE—Pressing Against the Gates of Heaven, Page 112 - #10.

PSALMS:

40:8 "I delight to do thy will, O my God: yea, thy law *is* within my heart," LESSON: 43—CONSENT—Love's Wisdom, Page 59 - #10 & LESSON: 206—YIELDING—A Moment of Choice Surrender, Page 220 - Definition.

46:10 "Be still, and know that I *am* God," LESSON: 13 (Student: Story)—CHRIST CENTERED PRAYER—Method, Page 24 - #21 & LESSON: 51—DIALOGUE - INTERNAL—Conditioned Response, Page 68 - #8 & LESSON: 64 (Student's Story)—EXPECTATIONS—Anticipations - Disappointments, Page 84 - #17 & LESSON: 76—GIFTS—Necessary Assistance, Page 98 - **GIFTS TO AWAKEN YOU:** G. & LESSON: 100—LANGUAGE—Expressions of Communication, Page 120 - **1. SILENCE:** A. & LESSON: 104—LISTENING—Guidance from the Spiritual Heart Center, Page 126 - Definition & LESSON: 158—SILENCE - OUTER & INNER—The Still Small Voice, Page 176 - #3 & LESSON: 188—VOCABULARY—Subjected to Change, Page 205 - #3.

51:10 "Create in me a clean heart, O God: and renew a right spirit within me," LESSON: 13 (Student: Story)—CHRIST CENTERED PRAYER—Method, Page 24 - #15.

56:2 "Mine enemies would daily swallow *me* up: for *they be* many that fight against me, O thou most High," LESSON: 60 (Student's Story)—ENOUGH IS ENOUGH!—Giving In to A Realization, Page 79 - #5.

57:4 "My soul *is* among lions: *and* I lie *even among* them that are set on fire, *even* the sons of men, whose teeth *are* spears," LESSON: 125—PIERCING—Attempts to Penetrate the Christ Amour, Page 145 - #1.

57:10 "For thy mercy *is* great unto the heavens, and thy truth unto the clouds," LESSON: 154 (Student's Story)—SERVANT I - THE CHRIST—The Christ Servant, Page 171 - #5.

62:1-2 "I am here Lord, I will wait for you," LESSON: 75—FRUSTRATION—Agitating Emotional Energy, Page 96 - #3 & LESSON: 129 (Student's

PSALMS:

Story)—PRAISE AND BLAME—Are the Same, Page 148 - **STUDENT STORY** - Paragraph 4.

62:5-6 "My soul, wait thou only upon God; for my expectation *is* from him. He only *is* my rock and my salvation: *he* is my defense," LESSON: 119—PATIENCE—Staying in Place, Page 141 - Definition.

67:2 "That thy way may be known upon earth, thy saving health among all nations," LESSON: 3—STRAIGHT GATE AND NARROW WAY—The Direct Path, Page 8 - #2.

71:5 "thou *art* my hope, O LORD GOD," LESSON: 83—HOPE—Fresh Water, Page 105 - Definition.

73:26 "My flesh and my heart faileth: *but* God *is* the strength of my heart, and my portion for ever," LESSON: 206—YIELDING—A Moment of Choice Surrender, Page 220 - #2.

77:6 "I call to remembrance my song in the night: I commune with mine own heart: and my spirit made diligent search," LESSON: 4—SPIRITUAL HEART CENTER—Best Kept Secret, Page 9 - #3.

77:7-8 "Will the Lord cast off forever? And will he be favorable no more" Is his mercy clean gone forever?," LESSON: 60 (Student's Story)—ENOUGH IS ENOUGH!—Giving In to A Realization, Page 79 - #6.

77:13 "Thy way, O God, *is* in sanctuary: who *is* so great a God as *our* God?," LESSON: 3—STRAIGHT GATE AND NARROW WAY—The Direct Path, Page 8 - #5.

85:11 "Truth shall spring out of the earth," LESSON: 181—TRUTH— Revealed Teaching, Page 198 - #3.

86:4-5 "for unto thee, O Lord, do I lift up my soul. For thou, Lord, *art* good, and ready to forgive; and plenteous in mercy," LESSON: 147—REMORSE—Deep Sorrow, Page 165 - #6.

PSALMS:

86:11 "Teach me thy way, O LORD; I will walk in thy truth: unite my heart to fear thy name," LESSON: 193—WALKING ALONE—Feeling Abandon by God, Page 211 - #9.

86:15 "thou, O Lord, *art* a God full of compassion, and gracious, longsuffering, and plenteous in mercy and truth," LESSON: 174—THOUGHTS - EMOTIONS - FEELING—Rising Vibrating Energy, Page 191 - #7.

90:1 "Lord, thou hast been our dwelling place in all generations," LESSON: 132 (Student's Story)—PREPAREDNESS-READINESS-WILLINGNESS, Page 153 - #5.

91:1 "He that dwelleth in the secret place of the most High shall abide under the shadow of the Almighty," LESSON: 28—BREATH—God's Life Force, Page 45 - #8 & LESSON: 202—*THE*"WORD"—You Are the "Word," Page 217 - #9.

91:2 "*He is* my refuge and my fortress: my God; in him will I trust," LESSON: 39—CONCENTRATION—One Pointedness, Page 55 - #8.

95:6 "O Come, let us worship and bow down: let us kneel before the LORD our Maker," LESSON: 204—WORSHIP—Spiritual Falling to Your Knees, Page 219 - #2.

100:5 "the LORD *is* good; his mercy *is* everlasting; and his truth *endureth* to all generations," LESSON: 181—TRUTH—Revealed Teaching, Page 198 - #5.

116:14 "I will pay my vows unto the LORD now in the presence of all his people," LESSON: 185 (Student's Story)—VALUING & APPRECIATING—What You Realize, Page 201 - #6.

118:6 "The LORD *is* on my side: I will not fear; what can man do unto me?," LESSON: 125—PIERCING—Attempts to Penetrate the Christ Amour, Page 145 - #4.

118:8 "*It is* better to trust in the LORD than to put confidence in man," LESSON: 8—ATTRACTION—Manifestations of Vibrating Energy,

PSALMS:

Page 17 - #17 & LESSON: 40—CONFIDENCE—Total Trust, Page 57 - #2 & LESSON: 125—PIERCING—Attempts to Penetrate the Christ Amour, Page 145 - #5 & LESSON: 185 (Student's Story)—VALUING & APPRECIATING—What You Realize, Page 201 - #9.

118:9 "*It is* better to trust in the LORD than to put confidence in princes," LESSON: 178 (Student's Story)—TRUST I - THE CHRIST—In The Christ, Page 193 - #8.

118:24 "This *is* the day which the LORD hath made; we will rejoice and be glad in it," LESSON: 78—GRATITUDE - EXPRESSED - SINCERE—Standing on Holy Ground, Page 99 - #15 & LESSON: 132 (Student's Story)—PREPAREDNESS - READINESS - WILLINGNESS, Page 153 - #7.

119:10 "With my whole heart have I sought thee: O let me not wonder from thy commandment," LESSON: 44—CONTEMPLATIVE—Accepts the Invitation, Page 60 - #2.

119:20 "My soul breaketh for the longing *that it hath* unto thy judgments at all times," LESSON: 106 (Student's Story)—LONGING—Inner Yearning For Your Reality, Page 128 - #7.

119:37 "Turn away mine eyes from beholding vanity; *and* quicken thou me in thy way," LESSON: 186—VANITY—Unnecessary Attention to the Physical Appearance, Page 203 - #4.

121:2 "My help *cometh* from the LORD, which made heaven and earth," LESSON: 78—GRATITUDE - EXPRESSED - SINCERE—Standing on Holy Ground, Page 99 - #5.

125:1 "Cease ye from man, whose breath *is* in his nostrils: for wherein is he to be accounted of?," LESSON: 178 (Student's Story)—TRUST I - THE CHRIST—Trusting in the Christ, Page 194 - #11.

126:2-3 "The Lord hath done great things for them. The LORD hath done great things for us; *whereof* we are glad," LESSON: 88—HUMOR—A Must on a Spiritual Journey, Page 110 - #2.

PSALMS:

127:1 "Except the LORD build the house, they labour in vain that build it," LESSON: 8—ATTRACTION—Manifestations of Vibrating Energy, Page 17 - #14 & LESSON: 55 (Student's Story—DRAMA—Hyper-Response/Reaction, Page 73 - #6 & LESSON: 64 (Student's Story)—EXPECTATIONS—Anticipations - Disappointments, Page 84 - #6 & LESSON: 99—KINGDOM—Natural Inheritance, Page 119 - #2.

129:15 "My substance was not hid from thee, when I was made in secret, *and* curiously wrought in the lowest parts of the earth," LESSON: 123—PERSON—A Separative False Sense of Reality, Page 144 - #4.

132:14 "This *is* my rest for ever: here will I dwell; for I have desired it," LESSON: 101—LAYERS—Three Major Layers, Page 121 - #6.

139:7 "Where can I go from thy spirit? Or where can I flee from your presence?," LESSON: 123—PERSON—A Separative False Sense of Reality, Page 144 - #3.

139:8 "If I ascend into heaven, thou *art* there: if I make my bed in hell, behold, thou *art there*," LESSON: 57—DRIFTING—Pulled Between Opposites, 75 - #6.

139:14 "I will praise thee; for I am fearfully *and* wonderfully made: marvelous *are* thy works; and *that* my soul knoweth right well," LESSON: 25—BELOVED—The One in the Many, Page 41 - #2 & LESSON: 202—*THE* "WORD"—You Are the "Word," Page 217 - #7.

146:2 "While I live will I praise the LORD," LESSON: 7—ATTACHMENT—"I, Me, My, Mine," Page 15 - #4 & LESSON: 129 (Student's Story)—PRAISE AND BLAME—Are the Same, Page 148 - #8.

150:6 "everything that has breath praise the LORD," LESSON: 28—BREATH—God's Life Force, Page 45 - #7.

*   *   *

PROVERBS:

3:5 "Trust in the LORD with all thine heart; and lean not unto thine own understanding," LESSON: 20—ANALYZING—Mind/Intellect's Nature, Page 37 - #3.

3:5-6 "Trust in the LORD with all thine heart; lean not unto thine own understanding. In all thy ways acknowledge him, and he shall direct thy paths," LESSON: 67 (Student's Story)—FAITHFULNESS—Standing Firm, Page 87 - Definition & LESSON: 183—TWO WORLDS, Page 200 - #3 & CONCLUSION - A CERTAINTY, Page 230 - Paragraph 8.

3:6 "In all thy ways acknowledge him, and he shall direct thy paths," LESSON: 3—STRAIGHT GATE AND NARROW WAY—The Direct Path, Page 8 - #9 & LESSON: 147—REMORSE—Deep Sorrow, Page 165 - #5.

3:7 "Be not wise in thine own eyes: fear the LORD, and depart from evil," LESSON: 200 (Student's Story)—WISDOM—Recognition, Page 216 - #2.

4:7 "Wisdom *is* the principle thing; *therefore* get wisdom: and with all thy getting get understanding," LESSON: 200 (Student's Story)—WISDOM—Recognition, Page 216 - #8.

12:15 "The way of a fool *is* right in his own eyes: but he that hearkeneth unto counsel *is* wise," LESSON: 60 (Student's Story)—ENOUGH IS ENOUGH!—Giving In to A Realization, Page 79 - #8.

14:7 "Go from the presence of a foolish man, when thou perceivest not *in him* the lips of knowledge," LESSON: 58—EGO—Bloated False Sense of Humility, Page 78 - #7.

PROVERBS:

15:2 "The tongue of the wise useth knowledge aright: but the mouth of fools poureth out foolishness," LESSON: 104—LISTENING—Guidance from the Spiritual Heart Center, Page 126 - #2.

16:1 "The preparations of the heart in man, and the answer of the tongue, *is* from the Lord," LESSON: 177—TRANSITION—Readiness Advance, Page 193 - #7.

16:18 "Pride goeth before destruction," LESSON: 135—PRIDE—Comes Before A Fall, Page 156 - Definition.

16:18-19 "Pride goeth before destruction, and an haughty spirit before a fall," LESSON: 87 (Student's Story)—HUMILITY—"Of myself I can do nothing," Page 108 - #7.

21:6 "The getting of treasures by lying tongue *is* a vanity tossed to and fro of them that seek death," LESSON: 58—EGO—Bloated False Sense of Humility, Page 78 - #4.

27:2 "Let another man praise thee, and not thine own mouth; a stranger, and not thine own lips," LESSON: 58—EGO—Bloated False Sense of Humility, Page 78 - #5.

*   *   *

ECCLESIASTES:

1:2 "vanity of vanities; all *is* vanity," LESSON: 186—VANITY—Unnecessary Attention to the Physical Appearance, Page 203 - #1.

1:14 "all *is* vanity and vexation of spirits," LESSON: 186—VANITY— Unnecessary Attention to the Physical Appearance, Page 203 - #2.

3:4 "A time to weep, and a time to laugh; a time to mourn, and a time to dance," LESSON: 79 (Student's Story)—GRIEF—Gut Wrenching Emotional Pain, Page 101 - #4.

5:2 "God *is* in heaven, and thou upon earth: therefore let thy words be few," LESSON: 188—VOCABULARY—Subjected to Change, Page 205 - #4.

5:3 "and a fool's voice *is known* by multitude of words," LESSON: 188—VOCABULARY—Subjected to Change, Page 205 - #2 & LESSON: 203—WORDS - WRITTEN - SPOKEN—Manifestation of Thoughts, Page 218 - #3.

12:7 "Then shall the dust return to the earth as it was: and the spirit shall return unto God who gave it," LESSON: 123—PERSON—A Separative False Sense of Reality, Page 144 - #8.

1:9 "All things were made by him; and without him was not any thing made that was made," LESSON: 47—CREATION—In the Light of Awareness, Page 62 - #9.

* * *

ISAIAH:

1:18 "Though your sins be as scarlet, they shall be as white as snow," LESSON: 26—BIRTH - DEATH—Imaginary Cycle, Page 41 - #6 & LESSON: 118—OVERCOMING—The White Robe, Page 140 - #3 & LESSON: 141(Student's Story)—RECONCILIATION - ATONEMENT - SALVATION—Acceptance, Page 159 - #9.

2:22 "Cease ye from man, whose breath *is* in his nostrils: for wherein is he to be accountd of?," LESSON: 76—GIFTS—Necessary Assistance, Page 98 - **GIFTS TO AWAKEN YOU:** C. & LESSON: 159—SIN—False Concept, Page 177 - #8 & LESSON: 178 (Student's Story)—TRUST I—In The Christ, Page 194 - #12 & LESSON: 185 (Student's Story)—VALUING & APPRECIATING—What You Realize, Page 201 - #8 & LESSON: 189 (Student's Story)—VOICES-THOUGHTS—Conditioned Imprints, Page 206 - #2.

6:8 "Here *am* I send me," LESSON: 37—COMPASSION—Meeting a Momentary Need, Page 54 - #5 & LESSON: 154 (Student's Story)—SERVANT I—The Christ Servant, Page 171 - #2.

7:14 "Behold, a virgin shall conceive, and bear a son, and shall call his name Immanuel," LESSON: 187 (Student's Story)—VIRGINAL CONCEPTION—Conception of Jesus, Page 204 - Definition.

9:2 "The people that walked in darkness have seen a great light," LESSON: 163—SOUL PAIN—Dark Days and Darker Nights, Page 180 - #3.

26:3 "Thou wilt keep *him* in perfect peace, whose mind *is* stayed *on thee* because he trusteth in thee," LESSON: 7—ATTACHMENT—"I, Me, My, Mine," Page 15 - #19 & LESSON: 158—SILENCE - OUTER & INNER—The

ISAIAH:

Still Small Voice, Page 176 - #6 & LESSON: 186—VANITY—Unnecessary Attention to the Physical Appearance, Page 203 - Definition.

26:9 "With my soul have I desired you in the night; yea with my spirit within me will I seek thee early," LESSON: 51—DIALOGUE - INTERNAL—Conditioned Response, Page 68 - #4.

30:15 "In returning and rest shall ye be saved; in quietness and in trust shall be your strength," LESSON: 51—DIALOGUE - INTERNAL—Conditioned Response, Page 68 - #7 & LESSON: 55 (Student: Story)—DRAMA—Hyper-Response/Reaction, Page 73 - #7.

30:21 "And thine ears shall hear a word behind thee, saying This *is* the way, walk ye in it," LESSON: 53 (Student's Story)—DISCIPLESHIP—Accepting the Hand of Jesus, Page 69 - #4.

40:8 "The grass withereth, the flower fadeth: but the word of our God shall stand forever," LESSON: 188—VOCABULARY—Subjected to Change, Page 205 - #7.

40:29 "He giveth power to the faint; and to *them that have* no might he increaseth strength," LESSON: 22—ANOINTING—Invested Power, Page 39 - #2.

41:10 "Fear thou not; for I *am* with thee; be not dismayed; for I *am* thy God: I will strengthen thee; yea, I will help thee," LESSON: 69—FEAR—Stumbling Block, Page 91 - #4.

41:13 "For I the Lord thy God will hold thy right hand saying unto thee, Fear not; I will help thee," LESSON: 67 (Student's Story)—FAITHFULNESS—Standing Firm, Page 87 - #9.

43:1 "O Jacob, and he formed thee, O Israel, Fear not: for I have redeemed thee, I have called *thee* by name; thou *art* mine," LESSON: 25—BELOVED—The One in the Many, Page 41- #4.

44:6 "I *am* the first, and I *am* the last; and beside me *there is* no god," LESSON: 170—SYMBOLS AND RITUALS—Forms and Practices, Page 188 - #4.

ISAIAH:

45:2 "I will go before thee, and make the crooked places straight," LESSON: 132 (Student's Story)—PREPAREDNESS - READINESS - WILLINGNESS, Page 153 - #6.

46:5 "To whom will ye liken me, and make *me* equal, and compare me, that we may be like?," LESSON: 36—COMPARING—Paper Credentials, Page 53 - #3.

54:13 "And all thy children *shall be* taught of the LORD; and great *shall be* the peace of thy children," LESSON: 103—LESSONS - MISTAKES & ERRORS—Manifested Guidance, Page 125 - #4.

54:17 "No weapon that is formed against thee shall prosper; and every tongue *that* shall rise against thee in judgment thou shalt condemn," LESSON: 178 (Student's Story)—TRUST I—In The Christ, Page 194 - #6.

55:8 "For my thoughts *are* not your thoughts," LESSON: 152—SENSI-TIVITY—Personal Acceptance of Criticism, Page 169 - #4 & LESSON: 198—WILL - FREE—Concentrated Mental Energy, Page 214 - #6.

60:1 "Arise, shine for thy light is come, and the glory of the LORD is risen upon thee," LESSON: 132 (Student's Story)—PREPAREDNESS-READINESS-WILLINGNESS, Page 153 - #8.

65:24 "And it shall come to pass, that before they call, I will answer; and while they are yet speaking, I will hear," LESSON: 8—ATTRACTION—Manifestations of Vibrating Energy, Page 17 - #21.

*　　*　　*

JEREMIAH:

29:13 "ye shall seek me, and find *me* when ye shall search for me with all your heart," LESSON: 4—SPIRITUAL HEART CENTER—Best Kept Secret, Page 9 - #9.

31:3 "I have loved thee with an everlasting love: therefore with loving kindness have I drawn thee," LESSON: 107—LOVE-GOD's—God's Nature, Page 130 - #3 & LESSON: 189 (Student's Story)—VOICES-THOUGHTS—Conditioned Imprints, Page 206 - #7.

* * *

LAMENTATIONS:

3:26 "*It is* good that a man should both hope and quietly wait for salvation of the LORD," LESSON: 83—HOPE—Fresh Water, Page 105 - #3.

*   *   *

EZEKIEL:

21:27 "I will overturn, overturn, overturn, it: and it shall be no *more*, until he come whose right it is; and I will give it *him,*" LESSON: 143—REFLECTION—God's Image, Page 163 - #8.

37:6 "and put breath in you and ye shall live and ye shall know that I *am* the LORD," LESSON: 28—BREATH—God's Life Force, Page 45 - #4.

*   *   *

DANIEL:

2:44 "And in the days of these kings shall the God of heaven set up a kingdom, which shall never be destroyed: and the kingdom shall not be left to other people, *but* it shall break in pieces and consume all these kingdoms, and it shall stand forever," LESSON: 99—KINGDOM—Natural Inheritance, Page 119 - Definition.

* * *

MICAH:

7:8 "O mine enemy: when I fall, I shall arise; when I sit in darkness, the LORD *shall* be a light unto me," LESSON: 163—SOUL PAIN—Dark Days and Darker Nights, Page 180 - #11.

* * *

HABAKKUK:

2:4 "Behold, his soul *which* is lifted up is not upright in him: but the just shall live by his faith," LESSON: 66—FAITH—The Kingdom of God, Page 87 - #6.

2:20 "But the LORD *is* in his holy temple: let all the earth keep silence before him," LESSON: 141(Student's Story)—RECONCILIA-TION - ATONEMENT - SALVATION—Acceptance, Page 159 - #10.

*   *   *

ZEPHANIAH:

3:17 "The LORD thy God in midst of thee *is* mighty," LESSON: 189 (Student's Story)—VOICES - THOUGHTS—Conditioned Imprints, Page 206 - #10.

* * *

ZECHARIAH:

4:6 "Not by might, nor by power, but by my spirit," LESSON: 152—SENSITIVITY—Personal Acceptance of Criticism, Page 169 - #14.

*   *   *

LESSONS CONTAINING NO
SCRIPTURE VERSES

NOTES

NOTES

NOTES

LaVergne, TN USA
03 February 2010
171985LV00004B/31/P